Vibrant Living

A live foods resource and recipe book

Natalie Cederquist and James Levin, M.D.

Illustrations by
Natalie Cederquist

Published by
GLO, INC.

First Edition

Published by

GLO, INC.

Worldwide Distribution by GLO, INC.

For information address:

GLO, INC., 2406 Fifth Avenue, San Diego, CA 92101

U.S.A. and Canada call 1-800-854-2587 toll free
All other countries call 1-619-233-9165

Printed and Bound in U.S.A.

Printed on Recycled Paper with Soya-based Ink

Library of Congress Catalog Card Number 93-78790
ISBN 0-9628698-2-1

Vibrant Living *was created by the authors of*
A Vegetarians Ecstasy and A Celebration of Wellness, to provide a valuable resource on live foods preparation for maintaining a diet dedicated to optimal health.

This easy to use, easy to read live foods recipe book includes:

- ♥ The benefits of living foods for optimal health and vibrant energy.

- ♥ Over 250 delicious recipes from Morning Meals to Vibrant Desserts.

- ♥ How to set up a live foods kitchen with food tips, shopping guides, and pantry items.

- ♥ All about food dehydration: the unique way to prepare live food burgers, chips, cookies, and crackers.

- ♥ How to sprout beans, grains, and seeds, turning them into indoor gardens of life.

- ♥ The benefits of soaking nuts, dried fruits, and sea vegetables.

- ♥ The basics on culturing seeds and nuts and how to make fermented yogurts and sauces.

- ♥ Easy ways to make nut milk, vitality drinks, and health cocktails.

- ♥ Sample menus.

- ♥ A cross-referenced alphabetical index.

We wish all of you vibrant health!

A Live Foods Story
of the Universe

Once upon a time there was a vast, unlimited, boundariless space that had two names for itself and for every place within that unlimited space and indeed there were an infinite number of those places with two names.

Each place was usually known as invisible and/or visible . . . depending upon how you looked at it. However, when one looked closely with awareness at each place or thing or life form or planet or animal or plant or person or tiny grain of sand, which were all new categories of names that were eventually given to each of the infinite "places" that were part of the "boundariless space," one discovered that the invisible and the visible coexisted at all places within the unlimited vastness. Indeed, all of the infinite places were the same regardless of their appearance or new name, they were "one" or UNIfied in their invisible-visible coexistence, so UNIfied that to keep things simple, the vast, unlimited boundariless space became known as the Universe.

In this Universe, the visible was one aspect of the invisible and was connected to all places where the invisible was present. Since that was everywhere, it became evident that everything in the visible and the invisible aspects of the Universe were interconnected. By this interconnection, one could observe that invisible events that affected any aspect of the visible, also affected all aspects of both the invisible and the visible.

Listening closely, one heard a vibration from the stillness of the invisible . . . a harmony of the wisdom of the interconnectedness of the life of this Universe.

When the visible or the material body of life in this Universe vibrates and resonates in harmony with the rhythm of the invisible, a rainbow appears across the entire Universe and whispers peace from this silence. This peace is available to us when we let the invisible wisdom of the Universe speaks through us—when the vibration of universal peace speaks in our daily lives with its voice of harmony and balance—we dance. This dance is the dance of Vibrant Living!

Vibrant Living

PART ONE

Vibrant Living

PART TWO

Recipes

To WGB

Thank you for being a continual source of enlightenment

*O*ur quest for more personal vitality accelerated while creating our last book, *A Celebration of Wellness.* We discovered that uncooked foods made us feel more radiant, and so we decided to explore a "Live Foods" diet.

Our 30-day commitment to live foods changed our minds that starchy root vegetables, legumes, and grains needed to be cooked to be well digested. In fact, we've found that we truly enjoyed grated raw sweet potatoes, sprouted barley, and other legumes in a uniquely different way than when they are cooked.

The physiological internal cleansing effect of live foods had a profound effect on our physical as well as mental and spiritual health. Meaning our body, mind, and spirit became clearer and more integrated as we felt closer to the Divine presence.

We began viewing "food" in terms of the quality and quantity of life force within the food itself. Living foods provide the maximum cellular vibrancy, "cooked" plant-based foods may maintain cellular functioning but do not enhance cellular rejuvenation or vitality to the degree that live foods do. "Live" foods *replenish* the body.

Live foods also lead us to a new level of culinary creativity. From our personal adventure into a "living" foods diet, we've discovered many wonderful flavors, textures, and tastes that we hope you, too, will enjoy.

May these unique recipes fuel your exploration into a more vibrant life!

We wish you the Divine good health that we are all meant to receive and may you realize that the quality of your health lies "soul-ly" in your hands.

THE CHOICE IS YOURS!

*When trying new ingredients,
please keep in mind that each person has different needs
and that some people have particular sensitivity to certain foods.
If you are not certain about whether any of the ingredients
mentioned in this book are right for you, please consult
with a nutrition expert or health professional to assure
yourself a proper diet in connection with
making any dietary changes.*

What Is Vibrant Living?

Vibrant Living is a lifestyle dedicated to the celebration of the totality of life. As with all lifestyle decisions, it is a choice. This choice is made easier for us when we become aware that when we are in harmony with the Divine cosmic vibrations of the universe we are experiencing the true nature of our being.

When we are born, if we were given an owner's manual for our body, it would reveal to us the intricate and miraculous biochemical requirements for each and every one of our cells to perform its Divine functions at their optimal efficiency. We would marvel at the way in which our body's cells, tissues, and organs were designed to resonate in harmony with the rhythms of the cosmos.

We would discover that the cosmic vibrations of the sun's precious, life-giving rays, and the natural clean air that we breathe, are transformed through the process of photosynthesis in plant life; and that these same plants are enriched by the earth's vital minerals and the water from the rains of the heavens. Just as the plants transform themselves in this bath of cosmic vibration, we too have the capacity to transform ourselves through a plant-based live foods diet.

We receive the direct impartation of the life force when our body's cells are operating on their fuel of choice . . . the invisible life-giving energy of the cosmos that has been transformed into plants. This impartation maintains the vibrantly dynamic bio-electric capacity of our cells and we experience the presence of the life force throughout our entire body, as the spirit of cellular rejuvenation has us resonating with all life.

This is vibrant living. This is the totality of our wellness. This is the celebration. The life force creates vibrant plants, which as a food choice create vibrant cells for vibrant living.

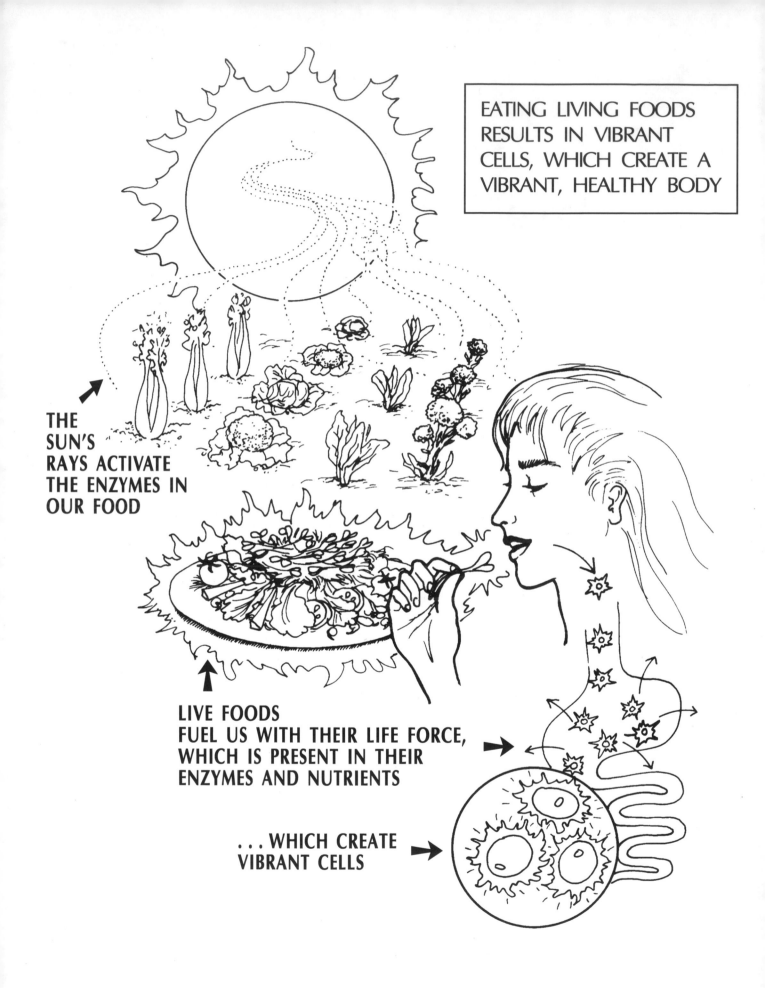

EATING LIVING FOODS RESULTS IN VIBRANT CELLS, WHICH CREATE A VIBRANT, HEALTHY BODY

THE SUN'S RAYS ACTIVATE THE ENZYMES IN OUR FOOD

LIVE FOODS FUEL US WITH THEIR LIFE FORCE, WHICH IS PRESENT IN THEIR ENZYMES AND NUTRIENTS

...WHICH CREATE VIBRANT CELLS

The Body's Energy Needs for Vibrant Living

Our marvelous bodies are energy systems that need vibrant sources of fuel to provide them with the necessary energy to perform their functions in an efficient manner. In the same way that an automobile's engine has been designed to perform at its optimum with just the right fuel mixture, so too do our bodies require just the right fuel mixture for their optimum performance.

The essential and most significant nutritional component found in the fuel mixture that is best suited for our daily diet is INVISIBLE and it is directly responsible for the regenerative and vitalizing benefits available from our live food choices.

The plant enzymes in our live foods are the physical manifestation of the invisible cosmic life forces that have been shown to replenish our body systems and reverse the process of cellular degeneration.

Only live, fresh, unrefined, biogenic, and bioactive foods (in eat-only-to-fullness quantities) re-energize us and prevent the depletion of our body's own life-promoting supply of enzymes. Traditional nutritional concepts are based on a limited awareness that sees the calories derived from carbohydrates, protein, and fats as the significant components of our food choices. Indeed, carbohydrates, protein, and fats are the primary physical or material combustible fuels from which our bodies derive their energy.

Although the body has tremendous adaptability and will function and survive on various mixtures of these primary combustible fuels, extended intake of a fuel mixture low in life-giving enzymes, high in fat (especially animal fats, dairy products, and excess saturated oils), will create sluggish, congested cells incapable of vibrant living. Diets high in animal protein and low in carbohydrates interfere with the inherent cellular wisdom necessary to direct the optimum functioning of our bodies' regenerative mechanisms. Whereas a fresh, uncooked, plant-based fuel mixture low in fat (10 percent or less of daily calories), high in carbohydrates (80 percent or more of daily calories), low in protein (10 to 15 percent of daily calories) allows the wisdom of cellular regeneration and vitality to speak and manifest itself in a vibrantly alive body.

A diet of live foods transfers the high quality invisible cosmic life force to our cells, for biochemical transformation into our lives as vibrant bodily function. Vibrant live foods create vibrant cells and a more vibrant you.

The Vibrant Living Spectrum

The illustration below shows the total body life force that you will experience based upon your food choices. As always, the Choice is Yours.

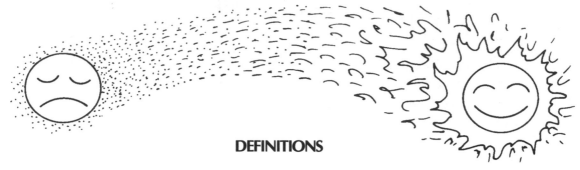

DEFINITIONS

BIOCIDIC FOODS
- Life destroying foods

BIOSTATIC FOODS
- Not life sustaining or life generating
- They diminish the quality of body functioning
- They are life slowing foods, which slowly increase the process of aging or cellular degeneration

BIOACTIVE FOODS
- Capable of sustaining and slightly enhancing an existing healthy life force.

BIOGENIC FOODS
- Life regenerating foods
- Cellular renewal
- Enzyme-rich
- Predigested proteins
- High in nucleic acids (RNA and DNA)
- Vitamin rich

EXAMPLES

- All processed foods
- All refined foods
- Foods with artificial additives and preservatives
- All cooked flesh foods

- Cooked foods
- Raw foods that are no longer fresh

- Live, uncooked, unprocessed, fresh fruits and vegetables

- The entire sprout family (sprouted grains, legumes, and seeds)
- Cultured and fermented foods (seed yogurts and cheeses, live sauerkrauts)

EFFECT ON OUR LIFE FORCE OR TOTAL BODY ENERGY SYSTEM

- Degenerates and disrupts the life force

- Our cellular energy is slowly depleted
- Our total body energy system must use its own energy in the assimilation of cooked foods

- The life force is slowly energized

- Cellular regeneration
- Increased vitality
- The life force of our body's energy system is increased

Resources: Cousens, Gabriel, M.D. - *Spiritual Nutrition and the Rainbow Diet*, Cassandra Press, 1986, and *Conscious Eating*, Vision Books International, 1992.

Szekely, Edmond - *Search for the Ageless, Volume Three: The Chemistry of Youth*, International Biogenic Society, 1977.

What Are Live Foods?

♥ Fresh, organically grown, uncooked fruits and vegetables

♥ Sea vegetables

♥ Raw, soaked, or sprouted nuts and seeds

♥ Sprouted seeds, grains, and legumes

♥ Fresh herbs and spices

♥ Fermented and cultured foods (seed "cheeses," "yogurts," and sauerkraut)

Living foods are abundant with all the nutrients we need for optimal vibrant health. In addition to carbohydrates, fats, protein, vitamins, minerals, water, and fiber, live foods also contain plant enzymes which are essential to our body's processes of cellular regeneration and digestion.

Why Eat Live Foods?

♥ To increase our energy, vitality, and to feel better than ever before.

♥ To cleanse the body of accumulated toxins and wastes.

♥ To obtain the highest concentration of vitamins, minerals, and nutrients from our foods.

♥ To receive the cellular regenerative benefits of live plant enzymes in our diet.

♥ To maintain our body's cellular physiology operating at its optimum nutritional and functional efficiency.

♥ To resonate in harmony with the Divine cosmic life force—the invisible essence of all life.

♥ To preserve our environment (land dedicated to plant-based agriculture requires less land, less water, less fossil fuels).

A Vibrant Living Model

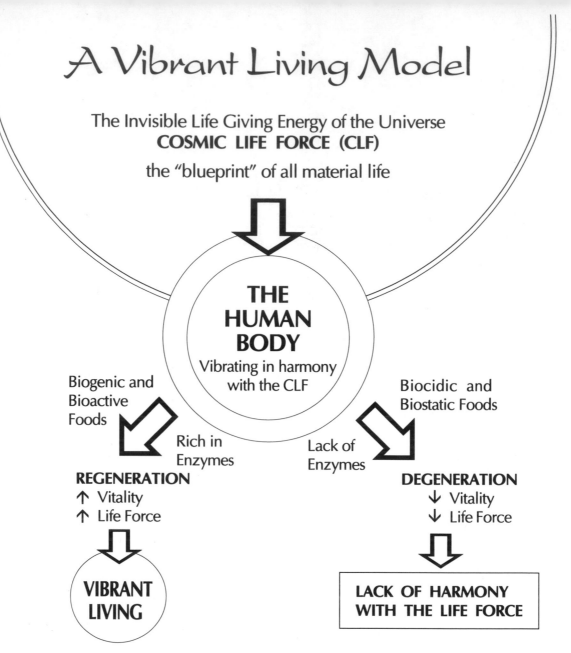

The Invisible Life Giving Energy of the Universe
COSMIC LIFE FORCE (CLF)
the "blueprint" of all material life

THE HUMAN BODY
Vibrating in harmony with the CLF

Biogenic and Bioactive Foods

Rich in Enzymes

REGENERATION
↑ Vitality
↑ Life Force

VIBRANT LIVING

Biocidic and Biostatic Foods

Lack of Enzymes

DEGENERATION
↓ Vitality
↓ Life Force

LACK OF HARMONY WITH THE LIFE FORCE

The plant food enzymes that are present in a Live Foods Diet are a material manifestation of the same invisible life giving energy of the Universe that gave us material life. They are the food messengers of regeneration and vitality, essential to the maintenance and enhancement of our own cosmic life force, which is our true source of vitality and vibrant living.

Enzyme-rich live foods enrich the bioelectrical potential of our body's cellular processes.

The amount and quality of the **invisible** cosmic life-giving energy present in our food is the most significant nutritional aspect of our diet. We are nourished by the invisible wisdom of all life which speaks through us as our body's physical and invisible vibration.

Live foods enable this voice of life to speak most eloquently.

Enzymes

Where there are live foods, there are life-enriching enzymes. Enzymes are essential in our diet for the optimum digestion and assimilation of all the life-enhancing and regenerating nutrients found in Mother Nature's live foods kitchen.

The enzyme energy pool of our bodies is limited in its supply, therefore if it is conserved by eating a diet of raw natural foods which are abundant with the enzymes required for their own digestion, then there is more unused enzyme energy available to us for other essential bodily functions.

All physical life processes are dependent on enzymes.

The cooking of foods (at 118°F or greater)* destroys the plant enzymes present in live foods, partially destroys most active forms of live food vitamins and minerals, coagulates food protein (making the protein more difficult to digest), and most important of all; cooked foods deplete our body's own enzyme-energy pool thus diminishing our regenerative capacity and life force.

WHY FOOD ENZYMES ARE IMPORTANT

♥ The body needs enzymes to enhance the process of cellular regeneration.

♥ Live foods that are enzyme-rich conserve the enzyme-energy pool of the body.

♥ Cooked foods that are enzyme depleted require the body to use its own life giving enzymes, thus diminishing the regenerative capacity of the body and over time leading to cellular degeneration.

♥ Our capacity to make enzymes is exhaustible.

WHAT PRESERVES ENZYMES?

♥ Our enzyme supply is increased by eating a live foods diet.

♥ Eating enzyme-rich cultured or fermented foods: seed "cheeses" and "yogurts," live sauerkrauts, and biogenic drinks.

♥ Biogenic foods such as sprouted seeds, grains, and legumes.

♥ Live enzyme supplements (wheatgrass juice).

♥ Fasting or liquid cleansing diets.

*Cousens, Gabriel, M.D., *Conscious Eating*. Vision Books International, 1992.

THE LIVE FOODS KITCHEN

Most food sources in the live foods kitchen are fresh, alive, and radiantly vibrant with pure energy. Dried legumes, grains, nuts, and seeds are storehouses of dormant potential energy (life force) quietly waiting to be activated through the addition of water, which turns them into vibrant sprouts.

We find it is best to buy these dried goods from bulk bins and stock up. Keep them in glass jars or sealed containers away from sunlight. Keep nuts and seeds in the refrigerator or freezer for the freshest storage possible. Make your trips to the vegetable stand more frequently to ensure the freshest organic produce. (The closer to having been in the Earth, the higher the life force energy they provide!) It is better to buy what you'll eat for a couple of days than to have carrots wilt or kale turn a light green from the loss of nutrients and life force.

Buy Organic

As with all food products, be sure to buy organically grown or pesticide-free food whenever possible. Kirilian photography has shown that organically grown produce has a more vibrant and radiant life force than chemically treated foods. (You become the life force vibration of the foods you eat.) Organic produce is sweeter, tastier, and richer in vitamins and minerals. Choosing organic foods is better for your health and for the future health of the Earth.

Fruits

Fruits are a great source of vitamins A and C, carbohydrates, natural sugars, fiber, and organic water. Fresh juicy fruits are cleansing and purifying; they contain simple sugars which are very easily assimilated. Fruits have a high water content, which in most fruits resembles the water ratio within the cells of our own body. However, too much fruit or fruit juice can produce too high a blood sugar, so moderate your fruit intake and drink plenty of filtered water when enjoying summer fruits. Be careful with non-organic fruits which have a stone pit (cherries, peaches, and apricots) for they are generally heavily sprayed with pesticides. Non-organic grapes are known to be one of the most heavily pesticide-sprayed fruits.

Dried fruits, rich in thiamine and iron, add variety to salads, nut milks, desserts, and sauces. Raisins, figs, dates, and other dried fruit can be soaked in filtered water overnight to soften them before adding them to recipes. Soaking not only helps when blending them, but also aids in facilitating their digestion.

Bananas are very versatile in a live foods diet. Buy bananas ripe (usually at a better price), then peel, chop, and put them into small freezer bags. Frozen bananas are staples for super creamy smoothies and non-dairy ice creams. Try dehydrating your own fruits for wonderful sweet treats. (See page 37, Food Dehydration.)

Vegetables

Use all fresh organic vegetables for a variety of nutrients and tastes. Vegetables are strengthening and fortifying. Roots, tubers, stalks, leafy greens, and vine plants all can be enjoyed on a live foods diet.

Sweet potatoes, yams, and jicama can be peeled and cut into sticks and eaten as a snack; or finely shredded and added to salads; or served shredded from a spiral cutter, creating long thin vegetable "pasta" to be topped with a delightful live sauce. Root vegetables provide live plant enzymes and are rich in complex carbohydrates and starches and they replace the cooked versions with much success. They can be added to stuffings, burgers, salad loaves, or crackers with much versatility. (We've discovered new snacking wonders in their natural raw sweetness.)

Broccoli, cauliflower, and other firm flowering stalk vegetables are delicious minced and tossed in a creamy sauce. Delicate leafy greens are best torn into a salad. Strong flavored greens such as kale, chard, and escarole are best shredded finely or minced. Try pureeing soft vegetables (eggplant, cucumber, tomatoes, or mushrooms) for live soups or sauces. You may wish to peel eggplants and cucumbers since their skins may have a tough and bitter taste, and may not breakdown well in a food processor or blender.

Many vegetables come with their own serving container. Scoop the seeds out of a bell pepper, tomato half, or zucchini and use the remaining shell in a unique presentation of stuffings or spreads.

Be creative! It is important to experiment so you can gain a greater working knowledge with food, and discover new and wonderful tastes. Experience the vibration of the live foods you are preparing!

Sea Vegetables

These nutritional powerhouses are worthy of being a regular feature in your meals. Sea vegetables are raised and bathed in the mineral-rich sea and contain collectively 56 known minerals and trace elements considered essential body requirements, providing high quantities of potassium, magnesium, iron, iodine, and calcium.

Another amazing substance found in sea vegetables is sodium alginate, which binds to heavy metals in our gastrointestinal track, forming a gel-like salt that has been said to eliminate radioactive and environmental contaminates through the feces. Seaweeds have been said to reduce these toxins by 50 to 80 percent!

Seaweeds are healing to the mucous membranes, promote healthy skin, aid in digestion and are said to enhance the mobility and flexibility of the joints. Use them in salads, as a condiment, in fruit gels (agar), as a holder for salad rolls (nori), or just enjoy them raw as a snack (dulse).

Here is a list of sea vegetables to keep in the pantry:

• **Dulse**—A burgundy colored red algae with a mild salty flavor. It can be eaten as is, or rinsed in filtered water to soften. Use in soups, dressings, sauces, and salads.

- **Nori**—A green algae pressed into sheets for sushi rolls. Use as a salad holder to wrap up a yummy live stuffing. Nori is higher in protein by weight than lentils and loaded with vitamin A.

- **Arame**—A thin brown algae, after it has been soaked it resembles angel hair pasta. Arame has a very mild flavor and makes for a delicious tasting salad ingredient. High in calcium, potassium, and vitamins A and B. Soak 10 minutes in filtered water to soften, then rinse and drain.

- **Hiziki**—Hiziki is thicker and shorter than arame and has a stronger flavor. Soak in filtered water 15–20 minutes to soften, rinse, and drain a couple of times before adding to salads. Hiziki is the seaweed that is highest in calcium.

- **Alaria/Wakame**—A pale green semi-transparent sea vegetable loaded with vitamins A, B, B$_{12}$, and E. Soak in filtered water for 20 minutes to soften, rinse, and chop into salads.

- **Agar**—A gelatinous sea plant that is sold in flakes or bars. A healthy plant-based replacement for gelatin in desserts. To make a gel, dissolve 3 Tbl. of agar flakes in 1 cup of liquid, bring it to a boil for 1 minute, then let cool.

Legumes

Legumes are the edible seeds within a plant's pod. They include peas, lentils, beans, and peanuts. A live foods diet includes sprouted legumes for increased protein nutrition. These sprouted powerhouses provide substantial amounts of protein, vitamin C, iron, niacin, thiamine, and riboflavin. Use them as an accent to salads, or in recipes "*Spicy Chile Beans*" and "*Black Bean Fiesta Salad*" (pages 207 and 191 respectively).

Sprouting awakens the life force and begins the enzymatic activity which turns a dried bean into a juicy plant, by breaking down its cellulose fiber. Once sprouted, their complex starches turn into simple sugars and their protein and carbohydrates convert to an easily digestible food source. Here are some favorite beans to sprout:

mung beans	**whole dried peas**	**aduki beans**
black beans	**garbanzo beans**	**lentils (green, brown, and red)**

We find lentils to be the easiest, quickest, and most delicious legume to sprout. Mung and aduki are also easy to sprout and make a great live bean chile. Garbanzo beans sprout well and their stronger flavor and firm texture seem to be enhanced by marinating them before eating. Other beans may not be digested well, so experiment for yourself or eat them in small quantities as an "accent" to a meal. See the section on sprouting for further information (page 32).

Grains

Grains are the seeds of various grasses and are considered to be the "staff of life"—especially if they are soaked or sprouted. Sprouting enhances many grains and turns them into delicious salad additions. Grains such as wheat berries are extremely versatile (from beverages to dehydrated delicacies), are easy to sprout, and are a cornerstone to a live foods diet. Try sprouting different grains for yourself and see what results you get. Be sure to include a variety of grains in your diet for their rich supply of B vitamins, vitamin E, phosphorus, proteins, and carbohydrates. Here is a list of some basic grains to try:

- **Wheat berries**—Hard or soft sprouted wheat berries can be soaked in filtered water for a delicious enzyme-rich liquid called *"Rejuvelac Lemonade."* (Its subtle flavor resembles unsweetened lemonade.) Sprouted wheat berries can be soaked further to create mock wines or champagnes. We have our version called "Sprouted Wheat Divine," instructions and other details can be found in the Cultured Foods chapter (page 157).

  Sprouted wheat berries are soft and chewy and can be eaten as is, put into a salad, or ground up and made into dehydrated breads, crackers, or cookies. Wheat sprouts can be planted in soil on a sprouting tray and allowed to grow into wheatgrass, which then can be juiced for a dynamic, rejuvenating, healing, and cleansing tonic.

- **Barley**—Chewy, sweet, and delicious after just one day of soaking in filtered water, yet acquires a soured flavor if sprouted further. Add to salads or breads (or try our *Mushroom Barley Pilaf* or *Oriental Barley Salad* on pages 94 and 95 respectively).

- **Rye**—Sprouted rye berries add a nice sour flavor to crackers and breads and are especially tasty with onion, dill, or caraway.

- **Brown Rice**—This grain needs a longer soaking time (48 hours) and yet still remains firm after a few days of sprouting. It can be ground and added to wheat sprouts when making crackers. Not a very palatable grain by itself.

- **Millet**—Although millet is an easy grain to sprout, it remains a firm kernel. Because of its small size, its crunchy, crispy texture makes a fine addition to salads or desserts. A few minutes in a steamer will render a crunchy sprout into a fantastically tender fluffy grain. Millet is a non-mucous-forming grain.

- **Corn**—After many attempts to soften both popcorn kernels and dried whole corn kernels, we discovered corn is a tough kernel to sprout. Our dream of a sprouted dehydrated corn tortilla has not been realized. If you have success with it, please let us know!

- **Oats**—We use soaked oat flakes extensively as a breakfast cereal because they are delicious and soften quickly when soaked in filtered water. Not only are they an excellent source of fiber, but they are a good source of calcium, iron, and vitamin A. Use ground oat flakes as a binder in vegetable loaves or desserts.

Nuts and Seeds

Nuts and seeds are extremely versatile staples in a live foods diet. They are a concentrated source of protein, unsaturated fats, B-complex vitamins, vitamin E, calcium, iron, potassium, magnesium, phosphorus, and copper. Both nuts and seeds can be eaten right out of the shell, soaked in filtered water or sprouted. Soaking nuts and seeds releases their plant enzymes and enzyme inhibitors (which break down their cellulose and makes them easier to digest). They become nutritionally enhanced and less fatty, and are therefore preferred over raw nuts or seeds.

Soaked nuts are used in making nut milks, seed and nut yogurts and cheeses, sauces, dressings, spreads, salad loaves, cookies, and other great taste thrills.

Finely grinding raw nuts into a powdery meal makes a creamier, richer sauce, nut milk, seed yogurt, or spread. Store raw nuts and seeds in the refrigerator or freezer to prevent oxidation and rancidity of their fat content. Here are some basic facts and tips on these staples:

- **Almonds**—Soak 12 hours in filtered water, then rinse and drain before adding to recipes requiring soaked nuts. You can store soaked almonds in a jar, with filtered water to cover them, for several days in the refrigerator. To sprout almonds, continue rinsing and draining for two more days until small white sprouts appear on the tip of the nut. Soaked almonds make delicious nut milk, nut crusts, nut cheeses, spreads, and cookies. High in calcium, magnesium, and biotin.

- **Cashews**—Finely ground cashews create the creamiest sauces, yogurts, and soups! They give a delicious richness to spreads and desserts, too. Since it is often difficult to find organic cashews, try soaking them in filtered water overnight to get rid of any chemical residue. You will also discover that the cashew oils float to the surface of the water. When drained and rinsed again, this method helps to defatten the nut. Cashews are high in pantothenic acid. They become biogenic when cultured into a nut cheese or yogurt.

- **Walnuts**—Soak walnuts overnight in filtered water and strain away the oils. Use in nut cheeses, sauces, nut milks, over salads, or in desserts. High in Omega 3 fatty acids (Essential Fatty Acids).

- **Pumpkin Seeds**—A small flat tapered green seed also known as *pepitas*. Their distinct flavor becomes even tastier when soaked overnight in filtered water. Use in salad dressings, nut milks, sauces, and seed loaves. High in iron, phosphorus, B_1 and B_2.

- **Sunflower Seeds**—A vitamin A and D powerhouse, rich in protein. The soaked sunflower seeds can be easily sprouted. Unhulled seeds can be planted in a garden flat tray and grown into delicious sunflower greens, ready to harvest in 6 days.

- **Sesame Seeds**—A calcium, magnesium, and phosphorus-rich seed. Enjoy sesame seeds as a ground meal, known as "raw tahini"; soaked in filtered water and made into seed milks, sauces, and "cheeses"; or simply sprinkled on foods. Add to sauces, dressings, salad loaves, or desserts.

- **Flax Seeds**—The best whole food source of both of the Essential Fatty Acids, linolenic and linoleic (LNA, LA). Essential to maintaining the most efficient bioelectric environment for optimum cellular functioning and life force regeneration. Grind up flax seeds in a nut mill to add to nut milks, sauces, dressings, or salad spreads. Or try soaking them in filtered water overnight to release their gelatinous properties, then rinse well through a strainer. Flax seed oil is a highly concentrated form of these seeds which are storehouses of the sun's energy. Adding a tablespoon a day to your nut milk smoothies, salad dressings, or *Orange Flush* will greatly enhance your vibrational health. Flax seed oil is best taken with a protein such as nuts or seeds, sprouts, or sprouted legumes.

Condiments

Here is a listing of our favorite condiments other than fresh foods such as onions, chives, ginger, garlic, chiles, fresh herbs, and lemon juice. Recipes for fresh salsa, pestos, and other savory condiments can also be located in the Sauces, Dips, and Spreads chapter (page 137).

- **Miso**—A fermented and aged soy bean paste which adds a savory salty flavor to foods. Miso has been enjoyed in Japan for thousands of years. It is high in B vitamins and enzymes. Add warm filtered water to miso and stir into a thin paste, add additional warm filtered water and you may serve it as a nourishing soup. Usually found refrigerated in two variations: as a mild mellow light-colored paste, or as a deep reddish-brown stronger flavored paste.

- **Nutritional Yeast**—Yeast flakes are sold in bulk bins in natural food stores. It is one of the best sources of B vitamins and minerals and is especially high in vitamin B_{12}.

Nutritional yeast is a wonderful source of vitamin B_{12} for vegan diets. Imparts a nutty, cheese-like flavor. Sprinkle on salads, add to dressings, smoothies, or salad loaves. One or two tablespoons a day makes for a vibrant "glo-ing" day!

- **Dr. Bronner's Mineral Bouillon**—A concentrated liquid soy broth. Rich in vitamin C, dulse, amino acids, and papaya enzymes. A hearty salty flavor.

- **Liquid Aminos/Quick Sip**—Both of these soy bouillon products have a lighter flavor than Dr. Bronner's. They are high in minerals. We find the Quick Sip to be saltier, and perhaps a bit more concentrated. (You may want to dilute it to your taste.) Use like tamari.

- **Tamari**—A naturally fermented soy bean sauce, aged to perfection. Tamari is more concentrated than soy sauce, which is usually made from wheat. Add to sauces, dressings, salads, or wherever a salty taste is desired.

- **Raw Tahini**—A sesame butter that thickens and enriches everything! It has been used for over 3,000 years by the Egyptians and other cultures in the Middle East. Use tahini instead of vegetable oil in a salad dressing, or add to make creamier soups, spreads, or desserts. It is also high in fat, yet gives a unique flavor and texture to meals.

- **Sauerkraut**—Naturally fermented sliced cabbage provides beneficial enzymes and friendly bacteria that aid in digestion. Try sauerkraut juice for a terrific cleanser. Opt for the organic no salt or low sodium sauerkraut. See recipes on page 162.

Vegetable Oils

Occasionally we use natural vegetable oils on our salads to get an extra supply of Essential Fatty Acids, or to impart a nice rich flavor.

The Essential Fatty Acids (EFA's) are Linoleic Acid (Omega 6) and Linolenic Acid (Omega 3), "essential" because the body does not manufacture them and must receive them from the food we eat. The EFA's are essential to maintaining the most efficient bioelectric environment for optimum cellular functioning and life force regeneration.

The highest quality and richest source for these EFA's is cold pressed, organic flax seed oil. Barlean's Organic Oils makes a wonderful flax oil rich in Lignans (which are said to enhance the functioning of the immune system). Flax oil is endorsed by Dr. Johanna Budwig, Ph.D.; a highly respected German researcher in alternative medicine, well known for her lifelong research on fats and oils and their effect on human health.

Other vegetable oils we use are cold pressed extra virgin pure olive oil or sesame oil. Use vegetable oils that are organically grown and stored in a brown (light proof, airtight) bottle or can. Oils are extremely sensitive to the oxidizing effect of sunlight and air, and will loose their freshness quickly if not stored in this manner.

If you prefer not to use any *added* vegetable oils in your diet, feel free to substitute raw tahini; or blend soaked cashews with a bit of filtered water, to replace the oil in the recipes that call for it.

Sweeteners

Here is a list of sweeteners to use in creating desserts or sweet sauces.

- **Date Syrup**—Blend soaked dates with their soak water (filtered) into a thick syrup.

- **Maple Syrup**—Extracted from the sap of a maple tree. Buy unrefined dark syrup.

- **Barley Malt/Rice Syrup**—Naturally sweet extracts from barley and rice that are super sticky, not as sweet as fruit sweeteners or maple syrup.

- **Frozen Juice Concentrates**—Organic juice preferred; look for pineapple, apple, or orange. Store in the freezer. A little goes a long way because these are concentrated.

- **Dried Fruit Purees**—A wonderful puree is made from soaking dried raisins, apricots, prunes, and figs in filtered water; then blending the soaked fruits with filtered water, juice, or their soak water. Use dried fruits alone or in combinations.

- **Bananas**—Fresh or frozen. A little goes a long way because bananas have a rich flavor that tends to overpower other ingredients.

   A word about honey . . . Because our *Vibrant Living Recipe Book* is about plant-based foods, we only use plant-based sweeteners in our recipes. Since honey is an animal-based sweetener, it is not included.

Food Preparation Machines

Here is a list of food preparation machines that will enrich your live foods culinary experience. Textures are important to keeping a live foods diet exciting and interesting.

- **Blender**—A classic kitchen helper which blends, purees, and mixes sauces, salad dressings, and drinks. For a longer kitchen use, buy a blender with sturdy stainless steel blades, rather than plastic fittings.

- **Cook Help**—A hand crank slicing gadget that creates long "spaghetti" style shapes out of vegetables: potatoes, carrots, apples, beets, or daikon radishes. Can be used to create fun shoestring or ribbon shapes, resembling a colorful fluffy veggie confetti. A very easy gadget to use that requires no electricity or batteries. Cook Help by Beriner is available through Soko Hardware in San Francisco.

• **Food Dehydrator**—An energy efficient "oven" that dehydrates the moisture from foods at very low temperatures, preserving vitamins and minerals. It works as the sun would, except it is conveniently controlled in the comfort of your own home. A food dehydrator will make "Live" breads, burgers, cookies, bars, fruit leathers, crackers, and other delights. See page 37 for more information. Foods only lose about 25% of their energy value when they are dehydrated, as compared to an almost complete loss of vibration and life force when cooked at 118°F or above.

• **Food Processor**—A powerful electric food prep machine that chops, mixes, grinds, finely grates, and slices in seconds. Use it to make "Live" soups, burgers, cookies, dessert sorbets, salads, and spreads. The most versatile kitchen machine around.

• **Seed/Nut Mill**—Pulverizes spices, seeds, and nuts into a fine powder. Use it for grinding whole spices (like cardamom pods, cumin seeds, cinnamon sticks, vanilla beans) for the freshest, most dynamic flavors. Quickly grinds nuts for a creamy nut milk, salad spread, or dessert.

THE FOOD CHOICES YOU MAKE
AFFECT YOUR LIFE FORCE!

COOKED FOOD = ENERGY LOSS

Cooked foods, refined and processed foods, all animal-based foods including dairy products, chemicals (alcohol, caffeine, tobacco) which take away from the natural energy of the body.

VIBRANT FOODS = ENERGY GAIN

Vibrant foods are fresh, uncooked fruits, vegetables, sea vegetables, soaked and sprouted seeds, grains, and legumes, enzyme-rich cultured seed cheeses and live sauerkrauts.

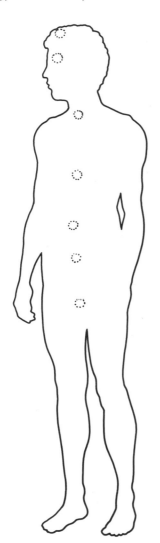

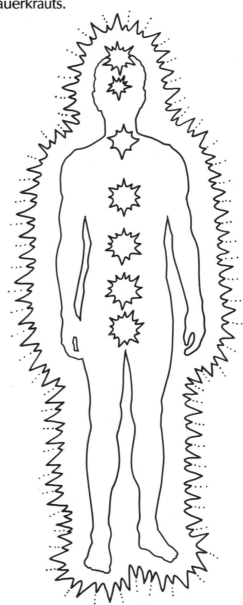

You can activate your natural Cosmic Life Force through choosing:

☑ A VIBRANT PLANT-BASED DIET   ☑ INCREASING PHYSICAL EXERCISE

☑ YOGA, PRAYER, OR MEDITATION   ☑ HAPPY THOUGHTS

Basic Live Food Procedures

WHY SOAK DRIED FRUIT, NUTS, SEEDS, AND SEA VEGETABLES?

Soaking dried fruit, nuts, and seeds in filtered water makes them more nourishing and easier to digest than when they are in their dormant dry form. When the nut or seed is immersed in filtered water for 6 to 12 hours, the life giving enzymatic process is awakened and the enzyme inhibitors are washed away. Once a nut or seed has been soaked it is biogenic and charged with life. Their plant enzymes help to pre-digest the fats, carbohydrates, and protein of the nuts and seeds, and makes them nutritionally superior than in their dry form.

We soak dried fruit to return them to their original plump juicy state. The higher the water ratio within a food source, the better it is for us.

How to Soak Dried Fruit
Place dried fruit into a bowl and cover it with filtered water. Then, let the fruit soak overnight or until soft. If the dried fruits are not organic, you may wish to drain the soak water and add fresh filtered water to the soaked fruit before you store them in the refrigerator. The soak water from organic fruits is full of vitamins and minerals and can be used in sauces or beverages.

Dried Fruits to Soak
Raisins • currants • dates • figs • dried apricots • dried apples • dried pineapple or papaya • prunes • and any other dried or dehydrated fruit.

How to Soak Nuts and Seeds
Refer to "Easy Soaking and Sprouting Procedures" on page 35.

Nuts and Seeds to Soak
Almonds • cashews • sesame seeds • sunflower seeds • flax seeds • chia seeds • pumpkin seeds • walnuts • pecans.

WHY SPROUT NUTS, SEEDS, GRAINS, AND LEGUMES?

The process of sprouting optimizes the nutritional content of a seed. Through sprouting, we awaken the seed's potential energy through an enzymatic transformation, preparing the seed for its ultimate fulfillment . . . life as a fully grown plant. The sprout's revitalizing life force is then transferred to our cells, which make sprouts the most dynamically alive food source available. Sprouts are a complete predigested protein which makes them easy to assimilate and digest, and they provide us with quick vibrant energy.

All nuts, seeds, grains, and legumes become enzymatically activated after soaking them 12 to 48 hours in filtered water; however, not all of them actually grow into a sprout. Most beans are easy to sprout, while only some of the grains, seeds, and nuts sprout. The air temperature and humidity of the room where you do your sprouting, combined with the freshness of the seeds, determine how long it will take for your seeds to sprout.

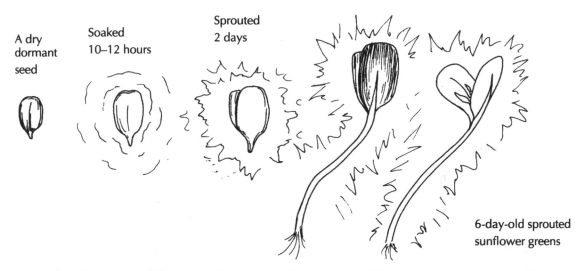

A dry dormant seed

Soaked 10–12 hours

Sprouted 2 days

6-day-old sprouted sunflower greens

After the basic 24-hour soaking time, let grains and legumes sprout in a dark place until they are softer and taste edible. The taste test is the best indication for when they are ready. Keep in mind when measuring out your grains and legumes, and selecting your sprouting jar, that grains and legumes will double in size after soaking and will triple in size after sprouting.

How to Sprout Nuts and Seeds: Refer to the "Easy Soaking and Sprouting Procedure" on page 35. Make sure your sprout jar has a wire mesh screen or cheesecloth top secured with a rubberband to prevent lose of seeds during rinsing.

Nuts and Seeds to Sprout
• **Alfalfa Seeds**—Use 1/4 cup of seeds for 5 cups of sprouts. After sprouting 3 to 4 days, place in a sunny area for chlorophyll rich green leaves. Ready in about 5 to 6 days. (Hulls will separate from the seed when the seed begins to sprout. During rinsing, scoop away any hulls that float to the surface. This reduces spoilage and improves taste and digestibility.)

- **Almonds**—Use 1 cup of almonds. White sprout tips appear after 1 or 2 days of sprouting.
- **Sunflower Seeds**—Use 3/4 cup of seeds. Ready after 1 or 2 days of sprouting.
- **Sesame Seeds**—Use 1/2 cup of seeds. Sprout 1 day.
- **Flax Seeds**—Use 1/4 cup of seeds. A natural mucilage will be released which surrounds the seeds, making them difficult to drain. We prefer just soaking flax seeds, but you may sprout them for 1 or 2 more days for a white sprout tip to appear.
- **Chia Seeds**—Use 1/4 cup of seeds. Ready in 2 days. A gelatinous seed when soaked, like flax seeds.
- **Garlic, Chive, or Onion Seeds**—Use 1/4 cup of seeds, or mix in with alfalfa seeds. Sometimes these can be difficult to sprout and may take 7 to 14 days, but they are delicious! (Other seeds to sprout are fenugreek and radish seeds.)

Nuts and Seeds for Soaking Only
Cashews • pecans • walnuts • hazel nuts • pumpkin seeds.*
*These can be sprouted for 1 day but no visible sprouts appear.

How to Sprout Grains and Legumes
Refer to the "Easy Soaking and Sprouting Procedure" on page 35.

Grains to Sprout
- **Rye**—Soak 30 hours since it is a hard grain. Sprout 2 to 3 days. 1/2 to 1 cup of dry berries for 1½–2 cups of sprouts. Use mixed with wheat sprouts.
- **Wheat**—Soak 24 hours, sprout for 2 days until sprout tails appear. Ideal sprout length is 1/4". 1 cup of dry berries yields 3 cups of sprouts.
- **Triticale**—Soak 24 to 30 hours, sprout for 3 days. Use 1/2 cup of dry berries for 1½ cups of sprouts.
- **Millet**—Soak for 24 hours, sprout for 2 days. This grain stays small and crunchy and is best mixed into other mixtures—not too tasty as is. Soak 1/2 cup of millet for almost 1 cup of sprouts.

Grains to Soak Only
- **Barley**—Sprouts are soft and chewy after 24 to 30 hours of soaking. Best when not left to sprout over 1 day. Use 1 cup of barley for a salad for 2.
- **Oats**—Soak whole oat groats 48 hours; soak oat flakes 15 minutes, or until soft, in equal amounts of filtered water to oats. Figure 1/4–1/3 cup of oat flakes per person.
- **Rice**—Soak 1 cup of rice 48 hours, may take up to 3 days to soften. Use in grain milks or crackers. Not very tasty by itself.

Legumes to Sprout
Most legumes are crunchy and delicious. The higher their water content, the easier they are to digest. Lentils and mung sprouts have the highest water content.
- **Lentil**—Our favorite! A juicy, delicious, and hearty legume that is easy to sprout. Ready in 3 to 4 days. Sprout brown, green, or orange lentils. Use 1/2 cup of dry lentils for 1½ cups of sprouts.

- **Peas**—Use whole dried peas. Ready after 3 days of sprouting, when white sprout tails appear. Use 1/2 cup of dry peas for 1½ cups of sprouts.

Beans to Sprout

We like to use a flax seed sprout bag when sprouting beans. The porous cloth of the bag allows total water drainage to prevent spoilage. Most beans are easily sprouted and can be combined and sprouted together in colorful combinations. Here is a list of the best beans to sprout. Kidney, Pinto, and other larger beans can be hard for some people to digest, so we've left them off our list.

- **Aduki**—A small red bean from China. Hearty sprouts are ready in 3 days.
- **Black**—A small South American bean. Sprouts are ready in 3 to 4 days.
- **Mung**—A delicious green bean that most people recognize as "bean sprouts." Sprouts are ready in 3 days, high in water content. 1/2 cup of dry mung beans yields over 2 cups of sprouts.
- **Garbanzo**—A round golden medium-sized bean. Soak for 48 hours, sprouts are ready in 3 to 4 days.

The Life of a Sprout

Having been released from their parched confinement in a storage container, the legumes breathe, awaiting life.

In jars of filtered water they soak, floating up to the surface, then slowly sinking back down as if in a bioactive dance. Inside the legume a complete transformation is occurring. The life force of the universe remembering a growth cycle: becoming, awakening, being born. These shiny wet seeds and beans, so beautiful in their containers, glisten like tidepool treasures.

Then it comes; the sprout, bursting out of the swollen bean. Blindly searching out, seeking the light, no longer a dormant potential. Growing, unfolding virgin leaves, root tails sweet and juicy. Yielding to life, givers of life, we savor their efforts. Mixed with vine ripe produce, they provide unsurpassed nutrition. A salad is their dream, until they blend into our cells and become one with us, imparting their biogenic electromagnetic essence to us in an organic transformation of the life force. We assimilate their vibrant nectar into our own vibrant living dance! Oh, to be a sprout, like a genie out of the lamp. Vibrant life is their gift. We are grateful . . .

Easy Soaking and Sprouting Procedure

SOAKING

STEP 1
Put measured seeds, nuts, grains, or legumes into a fine-mesh colander and rinse. Then put them into a glass jar and cover them with filtered water 3 to 4 inches above seeds. Use only unbroken whole raw nuts, seeds, beans, and grains for sprouting.

STEP 2
Let the seeds soak overnight, or for 8 to 12 hours. Legumes and grains soak for 24 hours. The filtered water bath awakens the plant enzymes within the seeds, triggering the life force's cycle of sprouting to begin.

STEP 3
Secure a wire screen mesh or cheesecloth on top of the glass jar to prevent seeds from rinsing away. Drain away soak water (and hulls), this will discard the enzyme inhibitors. Rinse the seeds with fresh filtered water, then drain again. You may opt to put legumes in a flax seed sprout bag for best ventilation and drainage. Rinse until the rinse water is clear. *This ends the basic soaking procedure.*

SPROUTING

STEP 4
After following the basic soaking procedure above, let your seeds, grains, or legumes rest in the glass jar on the kitchen counter (or other dark place) for 12 to 24 hours. Keep jars at a 30–45° angle for the best drainage, or use a sprout bag or basket. Repeat Step 3, rinsing 1 or 2 times per day until the sprout tails appear. Store sprouts in an airtight container in the fridge to stop the sprouting process.

(See "How to Sprout Seeds, Nuts, Grains, and Legumes" for more specific information.)

Culturing Foods

Culturing or fermenting a food is a food preparation process in which a ferment is created through the growth of friendly bacteria.

The ferment is produced from the breakdown of complex molecules in organic compounds. For example, airborne lactobacillus predigests the protein in a seed and nut sauce, creating a ferment. A ferment can be enhanced by the use of a previously fermented product, such as miso paste or *Rejuvelac Lemonade*, which are both loaded with friendly bacteria and plant enzymes.

Commonly cultured products in a live foods diet are seed and nut cheeses and non-dairy yogurts; these thick semi-solid foods are made from fermented seed and nut sauces. (Seed and nut sauces are created from soaked or sprouted almonds, cashews, sunflower, sesame or pumpkin seeds, and blended with equal amounts of filtered water until creamy.) Plant cheeses and yogurts are  highly charged with plant enzymes, airborne lactobacillus, vitamin B12, and other B complex vitamins; improving digestion and promoting healthy intestinal flora. They also provide a much enjoyed soft "cheese"-like texture and taste to a dairyless diet, and are especially delicious seasoned with herbs and spices.

Tasty live sauerkrauts are also enjoyed for their rich supply of enzymes and beneficial lactic acid, which assists in the development of friendly intestinal bacteria. Live sauerkrauts are purifiers.

Rejuvelac Lemonade is an enzyme-rich liquid cultured from sprouted wheat berries. This lemonade-like beverage assists in the digestive process and makes a refreshingly exhilarating drink. (Refer to the Cultured Foods chapter, page 158, for further information and instructions on creating your own delicious cultured live foods.)

Fermentation also means to excite and that is exactly how we feel when seeing a jar of seed and nut sauce thicken and bubble, developing a delicious gentle sour taste with a lemony aroma. The kitchen becomes a dynamic expression of nature . . . Oh, the wonder of it all!

Food Dehydration

Dehydration is the most simple, delicious, healthy, and inexpensive method of live food preservation. Moisture is removed from the food by a regulated flow of heat and air. Without moisture, microorganisms cannot grow; thus dehydrated foods are preserved for a long time while utilizing only a fraction of the storage space required for undried foods. The dehydration method of gently heating food to evaporate the moisture present and removing the water vapor formed, leaves the essence of vitamins, minerals, proteins, carbohydrates, fats, and plant enzymes virtually intact (with an estimated energy loss of approximately 25%). No other non-live food preparation method (boiling, baking, canning, etc.) is as nutritionally sound.

Dehydration also concentrates the flavor and nutritional essence of food.

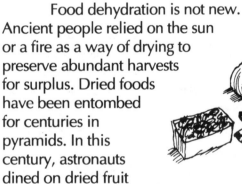

Food dehydration is not new. Ancient people relied on the sun or a fire as a way of drying to preserve abundant harvests for surplus. Dried foods have been entombed for centuries in pyramids. In this century, astronauts dined on dried fruit for dessert after walking on the moon! The space-saving ability of food dehydration, coupled with its condensed nutrition and flavor, leads us into the future.

Imagine the delicious tastes of your own sun-dried tomatoes, glazed banana chips, raisins, or sweet potato chips. In addition to drying your own herbs and spices, you will learn "Vibrant Living" recipes for making live food burgers, patties, cookies, crackers, chips, pizzas, and fruit leather.

Discover the food dehydrator and preserve the "nature" of your foods.

Ways to Line Your Food Dehydrator Trays

Many dehydrators do not come with a superfine mesh tray that will hold the "wet" mixtures of crackers, patties, or fruit leathers. Making your own liners is easy to do. Here is a list of liners to use.

• **Plastic Wrap**—Perfect for stick-free dehydrating of wet substances. Try to reuse the plastic wrap whenever possible since plastics are hard to recycle. Be sure to cut a center hole for the air to circulate.

• **Wax Paper**—Can be easier to handle than plastic wrap, although sometimes wet dehydrated mixtures may stick. Since this is a "mixed paper," efficient local recycling may not be available.

• **Brown Paper Bags**—Pre-recycled brown bags may be the "greenest" solution to use for a liner, however only firmer substances, like burgers, cookies, or herbs will work. After cutting out the shape you need, lightly coat the top side with a cold-pressed vegetable oil before using. This seals the porous paper and helps to prevent sticking.
Do not use with wet mixtures!

• **Cheesecloth**—This cloth works fine for thick moist mixtures, but it is too porous for wet mixtures. Once the cheesecloth is cut, it can unravel quickly. Stabilize reusable liners by sewing a seam around the perimeter of the inner and outer edge circles to strengthen them to withstand repeated washings. Buy the 100% cotton type, not the synthetic cheesecloth.

• **Unbleached Cotton/Canvas**—As with cheesecloth, you must sew a hemmed seam around cut edges to prevent unraveling to increase its usable life. You may also need to lightly coat the top surface with safflower oil to keep the mixtures from sticking. Use only with firm (non-liquidy) mixtures.

Keys to Staying on a Live Foods Diet

KEEP THINGS SPROUTING!

STEP 1

Sprouts are the powerhouse of a live foods diet because they are the ultimate live food, still growing on your plate. Begin soaking a couple of different seeds, nuts, beans, or grains every other day. At most, beans take 3 or 4 days to mature into sprouts, while barley takes only 1 day. This way you'll always have vital live foods on your table—whether it be a seed yogurt, lentil or mung sprouts, or just soaked almonds. You can prepare a fine meal adding sprouts to sliced or grated vegetables, or prepare a salad dressing or spread with the soaked almonds. Alternate your seeds and nuts with lentils and legumes. For instance, begin with soaking sunflower seeds, mung beans, and lentils. The next time soak almonds, alfalfa, and chick peas. Another idea is to make a bean mix (aduki, mung, and lentil mixture) and sprout them together, creating a "family" of your favorite sprouts!

You can also begin soaking sprouts for a specific recipe. Refer to the Sprout Chart to see how long the sprouts you need take to grow. For instance, you would begin soaking beans for the *Spicy Chile Beans* (page 207) four days before you want to prepare it. Once you get used to the rhythm of growing your own garden, you can grow sprouts anywhere you go!

BE SURE TO PLAN AHEAD

STEP 2

By thinking ahead, you can start sprouting something on Tuesday for Thursday's meal. Also you will need to prepare lunches or other snacks if you are working away from home. In a pinch, lunches can always be picked up at the store: a few bananas, or other fresh fruit, or a half of a melon; enjoy them with some dried fruit or fresh squeezed juice. Other away from home options are a salad bar or a fruit smoothie.

Nori rolls and lettuce leaves make wonderful salad holders for sandwich spreads. Fill them with tomato slices, avocado, sprouts, onions, or anything else you enjoy for a great lunch.

The key is to keep your favorite foods in the refrigerator so you don't run out. Hunger has a way of seducing you into eating non-living foods, so make sure you always have your stash of seeds or dried fruit wherever you go. You can keep a live snack filled container in the glove compartment of your car just in case.

For frozen desserts, you will need to cut up fresh fruit and store it in airtight bags and put them in the freezer at least several hours before you make a sorbet or non-dairy ice cream. These are all easy to do once you fill your heart with the rhythm of live food preparation.

STEP 3

KEEP FRUIT AT REACH

The brilliant colors and lovely shapes of fresh fruit have a very pleasing effect on us, sending us colorful messages of abundance. Knowing there is beautiful and vibrant food at hand makes it easier to enjoy your live food experience, and keeps you snacking on the optimum fuel for your body.

If you decide to do a 30-day program or if you just want to eat more live foods in your diet, this is a simple way to encourage your decision: keep a basket or bowl of fresh organic fruit at your work area and at home, and keep refilling it as needed.

STEP 4

TRANSITIONAL FOODS

If you really must have something warm, make a savory cup of broth or have a hot herbal tea. It's amazing how satisfying a warm broth can be.

Here is a list of some nourishing quick sips to enjoy:

• **Bronner's and Brewer's:** To a cup of hot filtered water, add 1-2 tablespoons of brewers (nutritional) yeast flakes and a teaspoon of Dr. Bronner's Mineral Bouillon (or to taste). Stir and enjoy. Other options are to add a dash of cayenne, pressed garlic, or minced chives or sprouts.

• **Natural Break Tea:** A convenient savory vegetable broth in a tea bag. Simply brew like tea. Imported from England.

• **Miso Soup:** Dissolve 1 teaspoon of golden miso in some warm filtered water in a mug. Add hot water to fill. Top with minced green onions, cayenne, and ginger if you desire.

Experiences Encountered on a 30-day Live Foods Diet

Everyone has their own unique metabolism, diet history, and relationship with food. Certain similar conditions may be experienced when trying live foods. Although we can only speak for ourselves, we hope you will find these shared awarenesses helpful in your own journey.

First 3 days:
An intense intestinal cleansing is being done. You may feel bloated or have increased bowel movements and gas. Your body is regulating itself to the increased supply of plant enzymes and fiber of these fresh live foods, and is cleaning out your colon of accumulated wastes. Your focus may be very physical; on the foods you are eating and not eating and how your body feels.

> **Suggestion:** *Brew a tea especially soothing for the above conditions from fennel seeds, ginger, peppermint, licorice, and anise. You may be able to find a tea called Digestive Tea or Polarity Tea with these ingredients listed. Drink lots of filtered water.*

Days 3 to 10:
You may experience heightened sensitivity and reflectivity. As your receptors become cleansed, your senses become heightened. You may experience more vibrancy of color, sounds appear sharper, foods have more taste and flavor. As you settle in to your new vibrant foods, eating becomes more fun, more dynamic, and more alive!

> **Suggestion:** *Begin writing a food or dream journal in which to reflect on and record your experiences. This is only for you to learn more about yourself. From our experience, magic generally happens when we undergo any dietary transformations. You may learn a great deal about yourself, your desires, your conditioning, and your society.*

Days 10 to 21:
Waves of subtle cleansing take place as you continue on the live diet. You'll feel lighter, brighter, your eyes become white and shiny, and your skin takes on a glow. This is similar to the effects achieved while on a cleansing fast. This may appear by day 3 or day 30, depending on how well you've taken care of yourself.

Suggestion: Take extra care in assisting your body's elimination. Take saunas or steam baths for a good cleansing sweat. Daily workouts assist in internal cleansing as well as keeping your muscles in shape. Get a massage, a salt glow, a facial, or a mud bath to assist in deeper transformation.

Days 21 to 30:

Gradually the focus changes from what you're eating to how you're feeling. You may not pay much attention to what you thought was so important in the first place . . . your diet. A light may fill you up so totally that you surrender to the gentleness of just being. This state is a truly spiritual awareness, for it is honoring the Divine within you. Your cellular structure is transforming itself, the light of the cosmos is circulating within you. Vibrant live foods are creating vibrant cells, which are creating a new vibrant you!

Suggestion: Know this presence within you as your own. Be mindful of what foods have contributed to this state of mind and being; and what foods cause you to loose your vibrancy and become dull. You are in control of how you feel. If you can feel this wonderful in just 3 to 4 weeks, just imagine how you might feel in 3 months, 6 months, 1 year, or 20 years! How well would you like to feel when you're 75, 80, or 100? The more vibrant live foods you include in your diet, the more vibrant you will feel.

Seven
Vibrant Things You Can Do to
Enhance Your Wellness

1 **LOVE YOURSELF**
When you love yourself, you are loving God, for you are a manifestation of God's love. Care for your body, be gentle with yourself, it doesn't matter what others think of you. All healthy practices will be of no use if you do not love yourself. Loving yourself is having self-respect, knowing you are a unique child of the Divine Plan. By loving yourself you see and honor the Divine within, which allows you to honor the Divine within others as well. All life is interconnected, love is the vibration of life's cosmic harmony.

2 **DEEP BREATHING**
Life is breath, for without breath, there is no life. Breath relates to the spirit, as in "God breathed life into all things." By focusing on your breath you will oxygenate your entire system. To achieve the benefits of deep breathing, follow your breath on inhalation as it first fills your lower abdomen, then your upper chest. Imagine this breath filling your body with love and purifying light. Then as you exhale slowly out your mouth, envision all the stale air and any negativity exiting out from your body. Continue this for as long as you like. Doing this daily will bring about amazing results. By focusing on your breath, you will quiet and still the mind, which is why doing these breathing exercises is a prerequisite for meditation.

3 **MEDITATION**
To meditate is to still the mind from all thought. Take time to hear the still voice of peace within. Feel life's love flowing through you, feel your radiance, feel at one with all. Let meditation take you to the fountain of the Divine, where you will drink of what your soul thirsts for. Use deep breathing as a means to focus your mind and prepare you for the peaceful pleasures that meditation brings. Daily meditation brings phenomenal results of inner peace and inner health. Meditation opens the door of life which leads to the realization of universal peace and harmony.

4 **EXERCISE**
Daily exercise will energize your body in addition to providing many other health benefits. By increasing the circulation of your blood, oxygen is carried to all parts of the body more effectively. This increased blood flow dynamically

nourishes and oxygenates your cells, making them (and you) very happy and vibrant! Exercise strengthens and tones your heart and muscles, burns fat, keeps you limber, and gives you energy and vitality.

There are two basic types of exercise: aerobic and anaerobic. Aerobic exercises require high oxygen consumption which brings cardiovascular benefits to the heart, circulatory system, and all the tissues and organs of your body. Running, walking, swimming, dancing, bicycling, and exercise equipment such as a stairmaster or a stationary bike provide great aerobic benefits.

Anaerobic exercise does *not* require high oxygen consumption, but will tone the body and increase lean muscle mass, while decreasing body fat. Weight lifting, carrying heavy objects, and various forms of physical labor are examples of anaerobic exercise.

For a better looking body with more vibrant and efficient cellular functioning in all your tissues and organs, combine stretching exercises with both aerobic and anaerobic exercise—and be the best you can be!

5 HAPPY THOUGHTS

Happy thoughts are unifying to your mind, body, and soul. They carry an uplifting vibrant energy. Happy thoughts radiate health, harmony, happiness, and success. Your thoughts determine your life, the types of relationships you have, and the experiences you encounter. If you want your life, your health, and your relationships to improve for the better, live your happy thoughts. Remember, you have only *your* thoughts to deal with, so why not choose a happy thought? Your thoughts create your life experience, a vision of celebration is the source of a life of harmony and bliss. Celebrate the wonder of it all and life will celebrate you!

6 CELEBRATE LIFE WITH KINDNESS

The gentleness you create by celebrating life with kindness, radiates into the world as a beautiful light; which in turn, fills your life with more kindness. Kindness is a way of saying "thank-you" to life.

7

Other things to do to promote wellness:

- Take a nap under a tree
- Sing a loving melody in your heart
- Associate with uplifting people
- Give your skin a body brushing
- Swim in the ocean, a lake, or a natural pool
- Rub your wet body with sea salt, then take a warm bath with essential oils

- Be joyful
- Get a massage or facial
- Walk in nature
- Smell a rose

- Be thankful for all of life's gifts

Vibrant Wellness
Begins with You!

*Please invest in your own vibrant wellness experience
by creating your personal list.*

**THINGS I PROMISE MYSELF TO DO TO PROMOTE
MY OWN VIBRANT WELLNESS.**

1 _____

2 _____

3 _____

4 _____

5 _____

6 _____

7 _____

8 _____

9 _____

10 _____

Recipe for Vibrant Living

Fills your day with zest and vitality, your face with a smile, your heart with abundant joy, and your path through life with meaning and fulfillment.

Amount to satisfy	**Live uncooked fresh organic plant-based foods**
An abundance of	**Clarity of thought**
An infinite amount of	**An open mind**
An unlimited amount of	**A heart filled with love and gratitude for all of life's gifts**
All you have	**Heartfelt appreciation for the Earth, the Universe, the well-being of others, and respect for all life**

Above all else, mix these ingredients with kindness, and serve daily in honor of the "Banquet of Life" that the Divine Presence has provided us with. Celebrate life and life will celebrate you!

Our favorite recipe,
with love,

Natalie and Jim

Liquid Delights

*The simplest recipes to prepare are found in our Liquid Delights chapter, beginning with **A Morning Cleanser**. This warm water and lemon juice cleanser is a great way to start your day.*

*From the zippy **Ginger Blaster** to a **Creamy Monkey Smoothie** your tastebuds will experience an array of delicious health building juice combos, nut milks, and sprouted drinks. Many of the Liquid Delights, once whipped up in a blender, become a meal by themselves.*

***Rejuvelac Lemonade** and other health building fermented drinks can be found in the Cultured Foods chapter (page 168). You will find unique sprouted wheat "wines" and other cultured beverages which contain beneficial plant enzymes to aid in digestion.*

So lift your glass as we toast to your good health!

Liquid Delights

♥ A Morning Cleanser 53
♥ Cranberry Gingerale 53
♥ Enlightn' Mint Tea 54
♥ Fresh Ginger Concentrate 54
♥ Ginger Blaster 54
♥ Gorilla Juice 55
♥ Hibiscus Cooler 55
Orange Flush 58
♥ Pink Lemonade 58
Romaccinos 60

Juice Combos

♥ Apple Lemonade 56
♥ Carrot Classic 56
♥ Carrot Cleanser 56
♥ Veggie Delight 56
♥ Watermelon Lime 56

Nut Milks

Almond Milk 57
Classic Cashew Nut Milk 57
Vanilla Milk 57

Smoothies

Creamy Monkey 59
♥ Froggy's Quantum Leap 59
♥ Hummingbirds' Buzz 59
♥ Orange Banana Flips 59
♥ Pineapple Date Shakes 59
♥ Pink Hawaiian 59

Drinks with Sprout Power

Sprouted Piña del Sol 60
♥ Sprouted Power Drink 60
♥ Sprouted Prune Whip 60
♥ Sprouted Tomato Patch 60
♥ Tropical Mint Julep 60

♥ FAT FREE

A Morning Cleanser

Begin your day by drinking a cup of warm filtered water with 1/2 a lemon juiced into it. This restores the acidic balance in your body, and is a very cleansing and purifying way to start your day.

Lemon juice flushes out impurities and excess mucus, cleans the liver and acts as a natural appetite suppressant. Wait 15 to 30 minutes before consuming other beverages or foods, so the lemon has a chance to do its magic.

Cranberry Gingerale

A zippy and refreshing cocktail.

1 c	**Natural cranberry juice cocktail**
1/3 c	**Lime mineral water**
1 tsp	**Fresh ginger concentrate**
	Ice cubes

Put ice into a tumbler, fill the tumbler 2/3 full with the cranberry juice, add the ginger concentrate and top with the mineral water. Stir with a swizzle stick, and top with an orange or lime slice on the rim of a glass.

SERVES: 1

Enlightn' Mint Tea

Fresh squeezed citrus goes well with mint tea, serve chilled or on ice.

6 bags	**Mint tea (approx. 4 Tbl loose tea)**
1 quart	**Filtered water**
3/4 c	**Orange juice (2 oranges)**
1/4 c	**Lemon juice (1 lemon)**
2 Tbl	**Maple syrup**

Sun Tea Method
Add the tea bags to the filtered water in a glass jar—let them sit in the sun for 5 hours or longer, remove the tea bags, add the remaining ingredients and then chill.

Stove Method
Steep the tea bags in a cup of boiling water for 10 minutes. Remove the tea bags, stir in the maple syrup, pour (or strain) into a pitcher, add the remaining water and juices— chill.

SERVES: 6

Fresh Ginger Concentrate

An easy way to have fresh ginger ready to use.
Prepare concentrate and then refrigerate.

1/2 c	**Fresh ginger root, peeled and chopped**
1 c	**Filtered water**
1/4 c	**Lemon juice**

1. Liquefy all the ingredients in a blender for a couple of minutes.
2. Strain the liquid into a glass jar and store in the fridge.

SERVING SUGGESTION
Use this in salad dressings, live soups or sauces—
or add to sparkling waters or juices. You can also add 1 tsp to hot
filtered water as a beverage to increase your circulation.

Ginger Blaster

An invigorating drink known to calm the stomach and increase the circulation. A
natural noncarbonated gingerale.

2 c	**Filtered water**
2 Tbl	**Fresh Ginger Concentrate (see above)**
1½ Tbl	**Maple syrup**
1 tsp	**Lemon juice**

Mix the ingredients together, then refrigerate. Serve well chilled or iced. You may also substitute mineral water for regular water for a bubbly drink.

SERVES: 2

Gorilla Juice

A high energy, nonfat, after-workout fortifier. The green color is due to the chlorophyll. Isn't it amazing that the gorilla's awesome strength and gentle nature come from a diet of only raw fruits and vegetables!

Per person:

1 c	**Filtered water**
1 c	**Pineapple juice**
1 tsp	**Spirulina powder**
	Dash of cayenne pepper (optional)
1 Tbl	**Lemon juice**

Blend well and serve on ice, or chilled.

SERVES: 2

Hibiscus Cooler

A hot weather tropical drink with a pretty ruby red color.

1/2 c	**Hibiscus flowers (dried herb)**
1/4 c	**Rose hips (dried)**
1½ quart	**Filtered water**
1 c each	**Orange and pineapple juices**
1/4 c	**Lemon juice**
1/4 c	**Maple syrup**

1. Add 2 cups of boiling water to the herbs, cover and let sit 15 minutes, stir in the maple syrup and strain the liquid into a pitcher.
2. Stir in the remaining ingredients, chill and serve on ice.

SERVING SUGGESTIONS:
Garnish with a pineapple wedge or orange slice if desired.

YIELDS: 8½ cups

Juice Combos

These juices can become your meals on cleansing days or fasts.

Apple-Lemonade

This is an intestinal broom. The flavor is bright, sweet and refreshingly tart. The lemon heightens the apple flavor, and acts as a cleansing agent for your liver and gall bladder. The apple pectin removes impurities from your digestive tract.

For 2 servings:

12	**Apples, juiced**
add 2-3 Tbl	**Lemon juice, to taste**

Carrot Classic

Carrots give you energy! They have a natural sweetness and are good for your digestion, eyes, skin and hair. An excellent source of beta-carotene.

For 1 serving:

8	**Carrots, juiced**

Watermelon Lime

Watermelon is an exceptional cleanser. Juice the white part of the rind as well.

For 1 serving:

8 oz.	**Watermelon juice**
1 Tbl	**Lime juice**

Carrot Cleanser

Carrot and apple juices make for a delicious, sweet and cleansing drink.

For 1 serving:

8	**Carrots, juiced**
1	**Apple, juiced**

Veggie Delight

This is a fortifying drink. It energizes, cleanses, and tones your system. Beet juice stimulates the liver, parsley purifies the blood and acts as a diuretic, spinach acts as a laxative and is good for the liver also. In combinations involving carrot juice, carrots should comprise at least 50% of the juice content.

You may also include tomato, cucumber, cabbage or bell pepper to this juice.

50%	**Carrot juice**
20%	**Beet**
10% each	**Spinach, parsley, celery**
Add	**Dill, cayenne, garlic, or lemon to taste**

Nut Milks

The healthiest nut milks can be prepared from soaked seeds or nuts, blending them in the blender with filtered water until creamy. Strain through a sieve two times before serving. A typical ratio of soaked seeds to water would be 1 part seeds to 4 parts water. Try making nut milks with walnuts, pecans, or pumpkin seeds and add a banana (or other fruits) and spices for fun sipping!

Almond Milk

A creamy white nut beverage sweetened with raisins; easy to make. Use like milk: over cereal, in smoothies, in baking, or just to drink. The process of soaking almonds activates its food enzymes, making its protein easier to digest. (If you like a sweeter milk, add 2 tsp maple syrup.)

3/4 c	**Raw almonds**
1/4 c	**Raisins**
5 c	**Warm filtered water**

1. Put the almonds in a glass jar and cover them with filtered water. Soak them for 18 hours. Put the raisins in a small bowl and soak them until soft.
2. Strain the almonds and raisins into a blender (reserve soak water for smoothies). Blend with 1 cup of warm filtered water for several minutes. Add another cup of water and blend for another minute.
3. Strain the almond milk into a carafe. (Use a fine mesh strainer, the more you strain the almond milk, the finer the milk will be.) Stir in the rest of the water, then strain again. Refrigerate. **Save the strained almond meal for breakfast, and top with sliced fruits.**

NOTE: Adding 1 Tbl lecithin granules will create a silky texture, and it also aids in the breakdown of fats and the maintenance of healthy nerve tissue.

Classic Cashew Nut Milk

A delicious, creamy dairy milk alternative. Pour over cereals or use as milk.

1/2 c	**Raw cashew pieces, finely ground in a nut mill**
1/2 Tbl	**Flax seeds, finely ground in a nut mill**
4 c	**Warm filtered water**
2 Tbl	**Maple syrup**
1/2 Tbl	**Lecithin granules**

1. Put the powdery fine ground cashews and flax seeds into a blender. Add 1 cup of filtered water and blend. Then add the rest of the ingredients and liquefy well.
2. Strain into a bowl through a fine strainer two times. Refrigerate. Keeps 3 or 4 days.

Vanilla Milk

Serve in sweet teas, over cereal, in fruit soups and sauces, or in smoothies.

1¼ c	**Almond Milk (page 57)**
1/2 tsp	**Vanilla bean, chopped**
2 tsp	**Maple syrup**

Blend in blender.

SERVES: 1

Orange Flush

This liver flush was designed by Dr. Stone and has super cleansing, strengthening and invigorating properties for your liver and whole system in general. You can add the garlic and cayenne according to taste. The Purifying Diet by Dr. Stone is a wonderfully gentle way to heal and cleanse. It consists of this flush every morning and eating only fruits and vegetables (raw or steamed), plus herbal teas throughout the day.

2 c	Fresh squeezed orange/grapefruit juice
1/2	Lemon, juiced
1 tsp	Extra virgin pure olive oil*
1 tsp	Ginger, chopped fresh
1	Garlic clove
Dash	Cayenne

Blend everything in a blender first on low, then on high till frothy. Strain into goblet.
*Try using flax seed oil instead of olive oil for your daily supply of essential fatty acids.

SERVES: 1

Pink Lemonade

For a thirst quencher, you can't "beet" it!

2/3 c	Lemon juice
3 c	Filtered water
5 Tbl	Maple syrup (or sweeten to taste)
1 Tbl	Beet, minced

Liquify in a blender. Strain through a colander into a pitcher of ice cubes and lemon slices. Chill well before serving.

YIELDS: 4 1-cup servings

Smoothies

*If you are in the mood for a light breakfast or lunch,
try one of these delicious blended drinks.*

Creamy Monkey

A banana smoothie at its creamiest!

1 c	Cashew or Almond Milk (page 57)
1	Banana, chopped and frozen
	Ice cubes
Option:	1/2 Tbl Peanut butter

Blend

SERVES: 1

Froggy's Quantum Leap

1 tsp	Spirulina
1½ c	Orange juice
1	Banana, chopped and frozen

Blend well.

SERVES: 1

Hummingbirds' Buzz

1/2	Banana
1/2 c	Frozen raspberries or strawberries
1½ c	Cherry cider or cran/raspberry juice
	Ice cubes

Blend well.

SERVES: 1

Orange Banana Flips

A wonderful morning drink.

4 c	Fresh orange juice
2	Bananas, chopped and frozen
	Several ice cubes

Put the ingredients into a blender and blend until smooth.

SERVES: 2

Pineapple Date Shake

A sweet delight!

3/4 c	Pineapple juice, unsweetened
5	Honey dates, pitted
1	Banana, chopped and frozen
	Several ice cubes

Blend well, adding ice as needed.

SERVES: 1

Pink Hawaiian

A tropical treat!

3	Strawberries, frozen
1	Banana, chopped and frozen
2 c	Pineapple juice
Several	Ice cubes

Puree in blender.

SERVES: 2

Romaccinos

A delicious cappuccino-like hot drink made from grains and Almond Milk; spiced with cinnamon and vanilla. A transitional drink for those used to drinking coffee.

2 Tbl	Kafree Roma or Pero
1 c	Hot filtered water
1/2 c	Almond Milk (page 57)
2 tsp	Maple syrup
Dash	Cinnamon and vanilla

Stir together in a large mug.   SERVES: 1

Drinks with Sprout Power!

Fortify your juices by blending them with sprouts.

Sprouted Piña del Sol

1½ c	Pineapple juice
1/4 c	Sunflower seed sprouts

Blend.   SERVES: 1

Sprouted Power Drink

For a lunch on the run or a power booster, try this blender special.

1½ c	Carrot juice
1/2 c	Alfalfa sprouts, packed
1 tsp	Lemon juice
1/2 tsp	Tamari or liquid aminos
1/2 Tbl	Nutritional yeast flakes

Blend well in a blender.

YIELDS: 1½ cups

Sprouted Tomato Patch

1½ c	Tomato juice
1/4 - 1/3 c	Alfalfa sprouts

Blend.   SERVES: 1

Sprouted Prune Whip

1 c	Prune juice (or 1 c filtered water plus 1/4 c soaked pitted prunes)
2 Tbl	Sprouted wheat berries

Blend.

SERVES: 1

Tropical Mint Julep

Protein packed with sprouts, a refreshing Southern treat!

2 c	Pineapple juice
1 c	Alfalfa sprouts
1	Banana, chopped, frozen Ice cubes
A few	Mint leaves

Blend in blender.

SERVES: 2

Breakfast Ecstasies

Breakfast is an ecstasy. It is the first meal of the day.
We offer an array of light fruit salads and hearty cereals to choose from.

For those who enjoy a substantial morning meal, we suggest trying
*the various fruit and grain müesli's, the **Caramel Apple Breakfast Pudding** or*
*the **Cinnamon Apple Cracked Wheat Cereal**. These soaked grain cereals provide*
you with the best easy to digest fiber-rich goodness necessary for
sustaining your energy throughout the day.

Persimmon Ecstasy**, **Sapote Exoticus**, and **Mango Magnifico
are exotic fruity puddings (topped with dried fruit and/or nuts) created to
lift your tastebuds to heaven.

Simple cut fruit salads for breakfast leave the palate clear
and the stomach soothed.

We also suggest you try the other fruit combinations in the
Salads of Life chapter. Or, whip up a smoothie from Liquid Delights for
*a simple morning meal. You may even nibble on a **Carrot Cake Raisin Bar** or*
*a **Sweet Energy Gem** from our Vibrant Desserts to complete your meal.*

A vibrant morning meal awakens your spirit for the whole day!

Breakfast Ecstasties

Amazing Grains

Fruitful Breakfasts

Fruit and Nut Delights

For other satisfying breakfasts, see also the Fruit Salads *section and the Smoothies in* Liquid Delights.

♥ FAT FREE

Apple Raisin Müesli

A hearty breakfast delight topped with a sweet raisin sauce.

3/4 c	Rolled oats
2 Tbl	Soaked flax seeds
1 medium	Granny Smith apple, cored
1 tsp	Lemon juice
Sauce: 1/3 c	Raisins
1/2 tsp each	Cinnamon and vanilla
1/2	Ripe banana
1 Tbl	Hot filtered water (or as needed)
Dash	Nutmeg

1. Soak oats in 3/4 cup of filtered water overnight in a medium sized bowl. Stir in the flax seeds.
2. Shred the apple using a medium grate disk in a food processor. Transfer to the bowl of oats and mix in the lemon.
3. Put the raisins and the next 5 ingredients into a food processor and pulse chop until blended thoroughly, pour on top of the müesli.

SERVES: 2

Caramel Apple Breakfast Pudding

A blended caramel sauce combined with fresh grated apples,
and then topped with raisins and almonds.

Caramel Sauce:

1/3 c	Sprouted wheat berries
1/3 c	Mashed banana
1/4 c	Sprouted or soaked almonds
3 whole	Dried apricots, pitted and soaked
4 Tbl	Apricot soak water
1/4 tsp	Cinnamon

2 medium	Granny Smith apples, cored and coarsely grated
2 Tbl	Raisins
2 Tbl	Soaked almonds, chopped

Blend the sauce ingredients. Divide the apples into 2 bowls and pour the sauce over the apples. Garnish with the raisins and almonds (or you may layer the apples with the caramel sauce.)

SERVES: 2

Cinnamon Apple Cracked Wheat Cereal

A scrumptious and easy to make breakfast delight, made from cracked whole wheat kernels, apple and cinnamon. We like it topped with a dried fruit puree, such as Prune Whip, but you may also top it with maple syrup, or a nut milk.

1/2 c	Cracked wheat (bulgur)
2/3 c	Hot filtered water
1/2 tsp	Cinnamon
1	Granny Smith apple, cored and grated
2 Tbl	Golden raisins
1/4 c	Prune Whip (page 234)

1. Put the cracked wheat into a bowl and pour the hot water on top of it, stirring together well. Cover the bowl for 15 to 20 minutes and let it sit.
2. Stir the cinnamon, apple and raisins into the cracked wheat. Divide into two bowls and top each serving with *Prune Whip*.

SERVES: 2

Fruitful Breakfasts

These can be quickly prepared for individual meals. Use lime or lemon juice or one of the following sauces to accent the fruit: Live Applesauce *(page 72),* Apple Creme *(page 234), or* Avonana Sauce *(page 106).*

Cantaloupe Cleanser

1/2	**Cantaloupe, seeded**
	Seedless red grapes, halved
	Lime wedge

Fill cantaloupe with red grape halves and serve with a wedge of lime to squeeze on top.

SERVES: 1

Golden Mandala

1	**Pear, cored and cut in 8 spears**
1/2-1	**Banana, sliced**
1	**Kiwi, peeled and sliced**
1	**Strawberry**

Place pear spears radiating out vertically from the center of a circle (like bicycle spokes), leaving a small area in the center for the other fruits. Toss banana and kiwi slices, then put them in the center of the circle. Decorate the top with a (whole or sliced) strawberry.

Maui Mango Delight

A simply delicious mango pudding topped with banana slices and raisins. A treat from the Islands!

2 ripe	**Mangos, seed and skin**
1/2	**Avocado, cubed**
1	**Banana, sliced**
1/3 c	**Raisins**

Stir together the mango flesh with the avocado. (You may puree them in a food processor if you wish.) Divide mango mixture into 2 serving bowls. Top each serving with banana slices and raisins.

SERVES: 2

Pink Tropic

1/2	**Papaya, seeded**
1/4 c	**Raspberries or strawberries**
	Lime wedges

Fill papaya with berries and squeeze lime on top, save one lime wedge for garnish.

Magic Müesli

A yummy breakfast oatmeal.

1/3 c	**Rolled oats**
1/2 c	**Almond Milk (page 57)**
2 Tbl	**Soaked raisins**
1/2	**Banana, sliced**

Stir together the oats and *Almond Milk* and soak overnight. Top with the rest of the ingredients, and add more *Almond Milk* if desired.

Müesli

Prepare the night before or let Müesli soak an hour or two before serving. The beneficial nutrients are preserved when whole grain flakes are soaked in this fashion rather than being cooked.

Per person serving:

1 tsp	**Apple concentrate or maple syrup**
1/2	**Apple, grated**
1/4 c	**Whole grain flakes (oat, rye, wheat or mixture)**
1 Tbl	**Ground flax seed**
1 Tbl	**Oat bran**
	Soaked raisins and almonds

Mix all the ingredients together and let them soak in either apple juice or soy milk. Spice it as you like with cinnamon, vanilla or maple extract.

SERVING SUGGESTION:
Serve with fresh fruit on top.

SERVES: 1

Multigrain Strawberry Müesli

A hearty morning cereal topped with berries and creamy nut milk.

1/2 c	**Multigrain flakes***
1/2 c	**Warm filtered water**
2 tsp	**Maple syrup**
4-5	**Strawberries, sliced**
2 Tbl	**Almond or Vanilla Milk (page 57)**

Cover the flakes with the warm filtered water in a small bowl. After 15-20 minutes, when flakes soften, add the remaining ingredients.

*Found in bulk bins at natural food stores. A blend of oats, wheat, barley and rye flakes.

SERVES: 1

Peaches and Creme

A delicious breakfast (or dessert) of fresh sliced peaches with an enzyme rich cream topping of almonds. You can also use Vanilla Cashew Cream (page 235) as a topping.

1/4 c	**Almond pulp (from making Almond Milk, page 57)**
1/4 tsp	**Vanilla extract**
1 tsp	**Maple syrup**
1	**Peach, sliced**

Put the sliced peaches into a bowl. Stir together the almond pulp with the vanilla extract and maple syrup, then spoon the mixture on top of the peaches.

SERVES: 1

Persimmon Ecstasy

A wonderful fruity breakfast pudding to enjoy in October through December when persimmons are ripe.

1 large	Persimmon, ripe (soft)
1/4 c	Banana, ripe, mashed
1 Tbl	Raisins

Stir together the persimmon pulp and banana and sprinkle with raisins.

SERVES: 1

Raspberry Almond Parfait

The almond meal from grinding soaked almonds is the basis for this hearty parfait.

1/2 c	Almond paste (from making Almond Milk, page 57)
1/2 c	Raspberries (or strawberries)
1 Tbl	Maple syrup
1 Tbl	Orange juice

1. Puree the berries in a food processor or a blender with 1 teaspoon of maple syrup and the orange juice. Stir the remaining maple syrup into the almond paste.
2. Alternate layers of almond paste with raspberry puree in a small cup, ending with raspberry puree. Enjoy!

SERVES: 2

Royal Applesauce

A delightful breakfast, lunch, and dessert.

3/4 c	Live Applesauce (page 72)
2 Tbl	Raisins
1 Tbl	Cashew pieces (soaked)
7	Banana Chips (page 125)

Put the *Live Applesauce* in a bowl, top with the raisins, cashews and *Banana Chips*.

SERVES: 1

Sapote Exoticus

Soft, ripe sapotes (custard apples) are a delicacy. Serve them sliced in a bowl with soaked fruits and nuts to make a wonderful breakfast.

3/4 c	**Sapote (custard apple), peeled and sliced**
2 Tbl	**Soaked raisins**
2 Tbl	**Raw macadamia nuts, chopped (optional)**
1½ Tbl	**Soaked flax seeds**
1 Tbl	**Sunflower seeds (soaked)**

Place sapotes in a bowl, stir in the remaining ingredients, saving the sunseeds for on top.

SERVES: 1

Sprouted Wheat and Date Loaf

An "Essene" style* bread, made from sprouted wheat kernels ground up with dates and orange juice and slowly "baked" to create a sweet moist loaf with a soft chewy crust. This one is "baked" in a food dehydrator.

2 c	**Hard wheat kernels, sprouted**
1/4 c	**Orange juice**
1/3 c	**Dates, pitted and packed**

1. To sprout the wheat, soften the kernels by covering them with filtered water for 24 hours. Rinse and drain twice a day for 1 to 2 more days, until white sprouts appear.
2. Put the wheat sprouts into a food processor or grinder and pulse chop until the kernels break up, about 1 minute.
3. Add the orange juice and dates and pulse together several seconds.
4. Spread onto a lined food dehydrator tray, dehydrate until dry on the outside with a moist cake consistency inside.

Keep refrigerated. Slice with a wet knife before serving.

*Essene bread is a slowly baked sprouted bread, using no flours, oils, eggs, or refined sugar; according to the *Essene Gospel of Peace*.

SERVING SUGGESTION:
Top with Live Applesauce *(page 72), banana, or nut butters for a delicious breakfast or treat.*

Vibrant Oatmeal

This is a simple raw müesli and is very good for you. By topping with live applesauce and some raisins or nuts, a splendid morning meal is created.

1 c	Rolled oats
1 c	Filtered water (or Almond Milk, page 57)

Live Applesauce

2	Apples, cored (peel if you wish) and chopped
2 Tbl	Filtered water or fruit juice
1/2 tsp	Cinnamon
1/2 Tbl	Lemon juice
	Dash of maple extract (optional)
Toppings:	Soaked raisins, chopped raw nuts of choice

1. Stir the water into the oats in a medium bowl. Let sit overnight to soften oats.
2. Pulse chop the apples, water, cinnamon and lemon juice in a food processor until a sauce texture is created.
3. Divide the oatmeal into 4 bowls, pour apple sauce on top of each, add some nuts and raisins if desired.

SERVES: 3 - 4

Salads of Life

Salads are the main creations of a Live Foods diet. In our Salads of Life *chapter, you will find two sections:* Fruit Salads *and* Vegetable Salads.

Fresh raw fruits and vegetables are vibrantly dynamic sources of vitamins, minerals, enzymes, fiber, water, carbohydrates, and protein; as well as being low in fat.

The English word 'salad' comes from the Latin word meaning salt, for vegetables are rich in organic salts.

Salads should be prepared from the freshest produce possible, preferably organic or homegrown.

Be sure to clean your fruits and vegetables well. Rinse leafy green vegetables, then spin or pat them dry. Scrub root vegetables with a vegetable brush rather than peeling them, which removes the vitamin-rich skin.

Envision your salads as a vibrant bouquet of Live Foods, arranging the varied colors that Mother Nature bestowed on them so that your salads are appetizing to the eye. Serve your salads as soon as they are prepared to receive their maximum nutritional and vibrational value. (The process of oxidation which diminishes the vitality of fresh fruits and vegetables is accelerated by the longer a prepared salad sits, and the finer your produce is shredded or cut.) Suggestion: include in your diet whole uncut fruits and vegetables (a carrot, an apple, a peach, or a banana), assuring you of the highest vibration that Nature has to offer.

The Salads of Life *offer the vitality of the Earth's bounty, served at Mother Nature's banquet. . . . So feast and be merry!*

Fruit Salads

♥ FAT FREE

★ This salad is fat free; however, the dressing has fat in it. Substitute a fat-free dressing of your choice for a fat-free meal.

Cantaloupe Flower Salad

A colorful and juicy salad. Serve on a shallow platter.

1	Cantaloupe, halved
1 c	Strawberries, halved
1/4 c	Walnuts, diced
1/4 c	Raisins
4-6	Endive leaves, sliced thin
2 Tbl	Lime juice
2/3 c	Blueberries

Seed the cantaloupe, then use a melon baller to scoop out the flesh, or chop flesh into bite-sized chunks. Toss in a bowl with the remaining ingredients.

SERVES: 4

Confetti Salad

A refreshing tossed salad of carrots, apple, celery, and currants, enhanced by mint and orange juice.

1 c	Currants
1/2 c	Warm filtered water
3 c	Carrots, finely grated
1/2 c	Celery, minced
1 c	Red delicious apple (1 medium), cored and sliced into small pieces
1/3 c	Orange juice
1/2 Tbl	Fresh mint, minced

1. Put the currants into a medium glass bowl, pour the warm filtered water on top and cover for a few minutes to soften.
2. Add the grated carrots to the bowl along with the apple and celery. Toss all the ingredients well.
3. Stir in the mint and orange juice. Chill.

SERVES: 4

Curried Waldorf

A crunchy, refreshing salad tossed with an Indian spiced Curried Pumpkin Sauce.

3	Celery ribs, chopped fine
2	Granny Smith apples
1-2	Pears
1/2 Tbl	Lemon juice
1/2 c	Raisins (or dates, chopped)
1/2 c	Curried Pumpkin Dressing (page 108)
3 Tbl	Minced pecans as garnish

1. Put the celery into a medium to large sized bowl.
2. Quarter, core and chop the apples and pears; add to the bowl.
3. Toss all the ingredients together and place on butter lettuce leaves, garnish with pecans. Serve extra sauce on the side.

SERVES: 4

Fresh Fruit Kabobs

Using the freshest fruit in season—springtime through summer —arrange fresh fruit in sections on a large platter. Serve on long bamboo skewers with lime wedges.

1	Papaya, cut into spears, without skin and seeds
2	Mangos, core, peel and chop
2	Bananas, peel, slice into 1/2″ thick pieces
3	Kiwis, skin and slice
3	Peaches or apricots, quartered
2	Oranges, cut into wedges, slice away peel
3	Limes, cut in wedges
	Bamboo skewers

Arrange the fruit on a large platter. Squeeze a few lime wedges over the papaya, mango and banana, dot the remaining limes around the platter. Skewer fruit like a "kabob," alternating the colors of the fruit.

SERVING SUGGESTIONS:
You can also create a "mandala" shape with the fruit.
Arrange in concentric circles by making the outer circle first, then working inward to the center. Banana and papaya do best on the outside of the "mandala," while smaller fruits go in the center.

SERVES: 4 - 6

Hawaiian Pineapple Boats

The pineapple shell becomes the serving bowl for this pretty party salad.

1 large	**Pineapple**
3	**Bananas**
3	**Kiwis**
18	**Strawberries**

1. Slice the pineapple lengthwise, cut the core out of each half. Cut out the pineapple into chunks. Set aside in a medium bowl.
2. Slice the remaining fruit, and add to the pineapple.
3. Fill the pineapple halves with the sliced fruit chunks and decorate the pineapple boats with the long spears from the pineapple cores.

SERVES: 6

Honolulu Tossed Salad

A tossed fresh fruit salad that you can improvise on, depending on what's fresh, sweet, and in season.

1 or 2*	**Papaya, halved and seeded, skinned and chopped**
2 small	**Bananas, peeled and sliced (try apple bananas)**
2 c	**Pineapple, chopped**
1	**Mango, cored, peeled, and chopped**
1/2 c	**Raisins**
1	**Apple, cored and chopped (skin if not organic)**
1	**Orange, chopped**
2 Tbl	**Lemon juice (or lime)**
1	**Kiwi, peeled and sliced—use also as a garnish**

1. Add fresh cut fruit to a large work bowl.
2. Add the lemon juice to the fruit bowl and toss all the ingredients with your hands. The lemon prevents the discoloration of the freshly chopped fruit. Chill.

*Note: Use a large "sunrise" papaya or 2 smaller ones.

SERVES: 4 as a main dish / 6 as a side dish

Independence Day Salad

A Red, White, and Blue Salad

1 basket   Strawberries
2   Bananas
1/2 basket   Blueberries

1. Slice the bananas and strawberries.
2. Toss the blueberries in a bowl with the sliced bananas and strawberries for a red, white and blue salute.

SERVING SUGGESTION:
Top with applesauce or with a sauce made from 1 Tbl maple syrup
mixed with 1 Tbl lemon juice, if desired.

SERVES: 2 - 4

Jicama Kiwi Salad

A bright and alive salad. A refreshing mix of juicy fruits with crunchy jicama root.
You can add grapes or raisins to this for added color and taste.

3   Oranges
3   Kiwis
2 c   Jicama (1 small to medium sized)

1. Peel and chop the oranges; peel and slice the kiwis; and peel jicama and shred in a food processor.
2. Put everything into a bowl and toss. Refrigerate.

YIELDS: 4—1 cup servings.

Orange and Fennel Salad

A light and juicy salad, refreshing in spring and summer menus or with spicy fare. Easy to make and simply delicious!

1 large	Fennel bulb
5 large	Oranges
2½ Tbl	Lime juice
1/2 c	Seedless red grapes, halved
1/4 c	Pomegranate seeds (optional)

1. Trim the top and bottom off of the fennel bulb. Set aside several green fennel sprigs for garnish. Quarter the fennel bulb and then slice it as thin as possible. Put the sliced fennel into a medium size bowl.
2. Peel, seed and cut the oranges into sections, then chop into smaller pieces. Add to the bowl.
3. Stir in the red grape halves and toss everything with lime juice. Top with pomegranate seeds and fennel sprigs.

SERVES: 4

Papaya Enzyme Facial

For wonderfully soft skin, try this effective facial:

Using the leftover peel of a papaya, rub the inside fleshy part of the skin over your cleansed skin. Let it dry into your skin, then rinse it off with tepid water.

Papaya Kiwi Salad

*A refreshing and delightful salad that also makes a great light dessert;
excellent for digestion.*

1 medium	**Papaya**
1-2	**Kiwis**
1/4 c	**Raisins**
1	**Lime, cut in half (juice one half, quarter the other half)**

1. Peel and slice the papaya into small spears; peel and quarter the kiwis.
2. Arrange the fruit on a beautiful platter and sprinkle with the raisins and the lime juice. Serve half the lime in wedges on the side for guests to use as a condiment.

SERVES: 2 - 4

Papaya Lime Salad

*This makes a delicious breakfast or lunch, rich in vitamin C, beta-carotene,
and the digestive enzyme papain.*

1	**Papaya, halved**
2	**Kiwis**
	Avonana Sauce (page 106)

Seed, peel, and slice the papaya into spears. Peel and chop the kiwis. Divide the papaya spears onto 2 plates, drizzle the *Avonana Sauce* on top and sprinkle with kiwis before serving.

NOTE: Chill fruit prior to serving for a cold salad.

SERVES: 2

Ruby Fennel Salad

This salad is so simple, yet fresh and clean tasting. The fennel and lemon lift your taste buds, and the grapes give a nice sweetness to the otherwise "rooty" beet.

1 large	Beet, chopped coarsely
1 large	Fennel bulb, chopped coarsely (save the sprigs for garnish)
1 c	Celery, chopped coarsely
1 c	Green seedless grapes, halved lengthwise
1/4 c	Lemon juice

1. Finely grate the first 3 items in a food processor.
2. Transfer to a medium bowl and stir in the grapes and lemon juice. Toss all of the ingredients well until evenly coated with lemon juice. Serve on a romaine or a wide lettuce leaf with a sprig of fennel on top.

Super "C" Salad

A sweet and juicy salad high in water content and vitamin C.

3 c	Orange sections, chopped
1 basket	Strawberries, sliced
3	Kiwis, skinned and sliced
1 Tbl	Lime juice

Toss together all the fruit and serve, or chill ahead of time before serving. The longer the salad sits, the more red it becomes from the juice of the strawberries. Stir before serving, because the juice will migrate to the bottom.

Wild West Pineapple Salad

3 c	Pineapple, core, skin and cut into chunks
1/2 c	Red pepper, julienne
1/2 c	Green pepper, julienne
1 c	Carrots, grated
1 Tbl	Lemon juice

Toss the pineapple, lemon, and peppers together. Top with grated carrots. Yippee ay yeah!

YIELDS: 5 cups

Yucatan Fruit Salad

A superb complement to Mexican main dishes. A refreshing fruity salad with a slight heat from the green chile.

2 c	Fresh pineapple
1 small	Jicama, peeled
1 large	Mango (not too soft), cored and skinned
1 tsp	Jalapeño pepper, chopped
2 Tbl	Cilantro leaves, minced (packed)
1	Lime, juiced
1 tsp	Poppy seeds

1. Chop the pineapple, jicama and mango, put them in a bowl.
2. Put the jalapeño chunks through a garlic press and press the juice onto the fruit, discard the fibers left inside the press.
3. Chop the cilantro leaves and add to remaining spices. Chill.

SERVES: 4

Vegetable Salads

♥ FAT FREE

★ These salads are fat free; however, their dressings do have fat in them. Substitute a fat-free dressing of your choice for a fat-free meal.

Salad Garnishes

*Here are some fun ideas for savory garnishes to sprinkle
over salads or to accent vegetable dishes.*

Avocado Balls: make them with a melon ball tool, use the small scoop.

Edible Flowers: whole nasturtiums, rose petals, Johnny Jump-ups, mustard
blossoms, violets. Try dicing them and then sprinkle them over a salad for a stunning
presentation. Be sure to use organic or unsprayed flowers. Flowers are a lovely addition
to fruit salads also.

Crumbled Herb Crackers: crumble crispy dehydrated crackers over salad.

Finely Shredded Roots: use the colorful yellow, red, and oranges of squash, yams,
beets, and carrots to bring greens to life as part of an edible rainbow.

Fresh Herbs: aromatic and tasty. Use minced or whole sprigs of cilantro, basil, dill,
oregano, fennel, parsley, mint, chives, etc.

Pepper Wedges: fill a pepper (green or red or yellow) wedge with a dressing, a dip,
or a stuffing.

Savory Seeds: use soaked sunflower seeds or almonds (chopped). Toss them in a
lemon juice/tamari mixture, or follow recipe on page 128.

Sliced Spicy Mushrooms: toss mushroom slices in a vinaigrette, sprinkle over salads
(or use a mixture of liquid aminos, lemon juice, and a dash of cayenne).

Speared Olives: slide a carrot or yam stick through a pitted olive.

Stuffed Olives: push a garlic clove or a jalapeño section in the center of a pitted olive.
Slice and sprinkle over salad.

Aramesk

A simple yet exotic salad of the sea, featuring Arame.

1/2 pack	Arame (seaweed), soaked (.88 oz)
1 c	Mushrooms, sliced
1/4 c	Carrot, sliced thin
1	Green onion, chopped
1 Tbl	Lime juice
1 Tbl	Sesame oil
1	Serrano chile, seeded and minced
2 tsp	Liquid aminos

Rinse the soaked arame in filtered water a couple of times (or you can put it into a colander and let cool filtered water run over it). Toss all of the ingredients together in a medium sized bowl.

SERVES: 2

Arugula Spinach Salad

A vitamin packed dark green salad. Use radicchio leaves as a "taco" shell to hold salad and dressing—eat as mini sandwiches.

1/2 bunch	Spinach, torn in half (about 4 cups)
1/2 bunch	Arugula, torn (about 1 cup)
5	Radicchio leaves
5	Button mushrooms, sliced
1 c	Alfalfa Sprouts
1 handful	Sunflower sprouts
1	Tomato, wedged
2 Tbl	Sprouted sesame seeds
1 c	Whey-Out Sauce (page 119)

1. Line a large platter with radicchio. Fill up the platter with the spinach and arugula leaves.
2. Place the mushrooms on top, add the sprouts around the perimeter and top with sunflower greens, tomato and sesame seeds.
3. Serve the sauce on the side.

Cabbage Cumin Slaw

This makes a large bowl of delicious slaw, accented with the flavor of cumin seeds.

1 small	Cabbage, shredded
1 large	Cucumber, quartered and sliced
1 large	Carrot, shredded
1/4	Red onion, shredded
1 Tbl	Cumin seeds
1 Tbl	Lemon juice
1/2 c	Tomato, seeded and diced
1 recipe	Cumin Vinaigrette (page 108)

Shred the cabbage, carrot and onion in a food processor. Transfer veggies to a large bowl. Stir in the remaining ingredients and refrigerate.

SERVES: 6 to 8

Chard Ribbon Salad

A deliciously healthy salad and a great way to eat vitamin-packed red chard leaves.

1½ c	Carrots, chopped and finely shredded
2 c	Red pepper, diced
2 c	Chard "Ribbons"
1/2 c	Red Rogue Dressing (page 115) (or use favorite vinaigrette)

1. Put the carrots and red pepper into a large bowl.
2. Rinse and pat dry the chard leaves. Trim out the chard stem in a "V" shape, 2″ to 3″ above leaf attachment. Stack 3 leaves on top of each other, then roll up tightly. From the open end, slice "ribbons" off as thin as possible. Unravel into bowl.
3. Toss all the ingredients together with the dressing.

SERVES: 4

Delphi Spinach Salad

A spinach salad topped with cucumber, tomato, red onion, and olives—perfect for outdoor dining. Top with seed cheese to resemble a classic Greek salad.

1 bunch	Spinach
1/2	Cucumber, skinned
Several	Cherry tomatoes, halved
6	Black olives, sliced
1/4 c	Red Onion Pickles (page 96)
3 Tbl	Sunflower seeds, freshly soaked
	Lemon wedges

1. Rinse, drain, and pat the spinach leaves dry and tear them into a large bowl or platter.
2. Add sliced cucumbers, tomatoes and the remaining ingredients. Serve with *Lemon Tahini Sauce*, page 144, or a salad dressing of your choice.

Fennel Cabbage Slaw

The fragrance of fresh herbs with the sweetness of fennel provides a wonderful combination.

2 small	Zucchinis
2	Yellow crookneck squash
2	Carrots
1	Fennel bulb
1/2	Head cabbage
1 Tbl	Fresh dill, minced
1 Tbl	Soaked sunseeds (optional)

1. Slice the zucchini in rounds, julienne the squash, thinly slice the carrots, and shred the fennel and cabbage.
2. Toss in a bowl with *Light Cucumber Dressing*, page 111, or a salad dressing of your choice, then add the dill and sunseeds.

Fiesta Coleslaw

Jicama, cucumber and fresh sweet corn off the cob enhance this "coleslaw" with a Mexican flair. An Avocado Sauce tops it off.

2 c	Green cabbage, grated (approx. 1/2 head)
2 c	Small red cabbage, grated (1/2 head)
1 c packed	Carrots, finely grated (2 medium)
1 c	Sweet corn, cut off the cob (1 ear)
1 c	Jicama, sliced and diced
1 recipe	Avocado Sauce (page 105)

1. If using a food processor, medium grate the cabbages; then change the blade and finely grate the carrots.
2. Transfer the cabbage-carrot mixture to a large bowl and toss it together with the remaining ingredients and the *Avocado Sauce*.
3. Garnish with tomato slices, cilantro and pumpkin or sunflower seeds if desired.

SERVES: 6 - 8

French Bean Salad

A beautifully colored salad of green beans, purple onion slivers and red tomato pieces; accented with garlic and rosemary.

1 c	Red onion, thinly sliced, then cut in half
1/4 c	Lemon juice
3 c	French green beans, trimmed and sliced
1 c	Tomato, seeded and chopped small (1 medium)
1 large	Garlic clove, pressed
1 tsp	Liquid aminos
Optional: 1 tsp	Extra virgin olive oil
3/4 tsp	Dried Rosemary, crushed fine
	Freshly cracked black pepper to taste

1. Put the onion slivers into a large bowl and toss in the lemon juice.
2. Cut the green beans on an angle, into 1˝ lengths. Add to the bowl with the remaining ingredients. Toss well and refrigerate for several hours.

NOTE: For added protein, add 1 cup sprouted mixed beans to the salad (Aduki, mung or a lentil combination)

YIELDS: 4 cups

Grated Beet Salad

Figure 1 beet per person. This salad is simple and refreshing!

2 c	Grated beets (4)
3 Tbl	Lemon or lime juice (or brown rice vinegar)
1½ Tbl	Fresh dill, chopped
	Add fresh green peas for a varied salad

Grate beets finely (a fine-shred food processor blade works the best), toss with lemon or lime juice—chill.

SERVES: 4

Hot House Cucumber Almond Salad

A crisp refreshing salad of cucumbers, green onions, lemon, almonds and dill.

1	Hot house cucumber (skinned if not organic)
1/3 c	Green onion, minced
1/4 c	Almonds, sliced
Sauce: 3 Tbl	Lemon juice
1 tsp	Almond butter
1/2 tsp	Liquid aminos
1 tsp	Dill weed
1 or 2 tsp	Maple syrup

Halve the cucumbers lengthwise and then slice them thin. Stir them together with the onions and almonds. Blend the sauce ingredients and toss the sauce into the cucumbers. Refrigerate.

SERVES: 2 - 3

Jicama Sticks

Refreshing, crunchy and sweet. Jicama is a root used frequently in Mexican cuisine. Served here traditionally, with lime and a dash of chile pepper.

1	Jicama, peeled
2	Limes, divided use
1½ tsp	Chile powder
1/8 tsp	Sea salt

1. Slice jicama into sticks, about 1/2˝ thick by 2˝ to 3˝ long.
2. Juice 1 lime and mix into the jicama in a medium bowl.
3. Mix the spices together and sprinkle on a plate. Dip one end of jicama in spices and place on a platter with lime wedges. Serve chilled.

Mandala Salads

The visual arrangement of salads can be designed to symbolize the wheels of the universe. Constructing symmetrical, artful salads can be a fun way to be creative and is exceptionally delightful to delve into. These are our favorite salads.

Traditionally, mandalas have been created by native peoples as an aid to meditation and as a vehicle for teaching their spiritual oneness with all. Creating mandalas is a ceremony in itself. See it as a sacred presentation for yourself and loved ones, each molecule of food being a crystal of love.

For a vegetable mandala, begin with a large platter or dish, and place spinach, lettuce or beet greens around the perimeter. Continue whirling this spiral flower with the vegetables that please you, such as, finely shredded roots, julienne zucchinis, cucumber spears and sprouts. End in the center with something beautiful, like a radish "flower". For a fruit mandala, place lettuce leaves around perimeter, spiral fresh fruits in a pleasing pattern, and decorate with soaked dried fruit and nuts.

As you create a beautiful salad, remember that we too create our lives; what a gift!

Marinated Cucumbers

    2 c   **Cucumbers, skinned and sliced thin**
    1   **Red onion, sliced thin**
  1/2 c   **Red Rogue Dressing (page 115)**

Toss together and let chill overnight or longer.

Marvelous Orange Asparagus Salad

Young tender asparagus is delicious uncooked. It has a subtle flavor that is enhanced with a citrus dressing.

  1 bunch   **Young thin asparagus**
  Several   **Bibb lettuce leaves, washed and dried**
        2   **Oranges, peeled, seeded, and diced small**
    1/4 c   **Red pepper, finely minced**
    1/3 c   **Orange Miso Dressing (page 113), or vinaigrette**

1. Trim the asparagus by cutting off the tough fibrous ends. You may wish to peel away the outer skin (lower 1˝ of stem) if it is tough. Lay the asparagus on a plate of bibb lettuce leaves.
2. Toss the oranges and red pepper together, then sprinkle over the asparagus spears.
3. Drizzle the dressing on top of the asparagus and orange mixture.

SERVES: 2 - 4

Minced Cauliflower Salad

Dill, celery and lemon make nice companions for this minced cauliflower salad.

2½ c	Cauliflower, finely minced
1/2 c	Cauliflower florettes
1/2 c each	Red onion and bell pepper, chopped
1 tsp	Liquid aminos
1/4 c	Lemon juice
1 tsp	Dill weed
1 c	Celery, minced

Combine in a bowl and refrigerate.

YIELDS: 5 cups

Mushroom Barley Pilaf

A wonderful sprouted barley salad, chewy, moist, and flavorful. Button mushrooms, green onions, and garlic add additional color, texture, and flavor. The blended sauce consists of chopped tomatoes, seasoned with miso and tahini.

Pilaf: 3/4 c	Button mushrooms, quartered
3/4 c	Sprouted barley*
1/4 c	Green onions, minced (green part)
1/2 to 1 tsp	Garlic, minced
2 tsp	Lemon juice
Sauce: 1/4 c	Tomato, chopped
2 Tbl	Filtered water
1 tsp	Miso
1 tsp	Tahini
	Cracked pepper to taste

1. Put the pilaf ingredients into a bowl.
2. Blend the sauce in a blender, then pour over the pilaf.
3. Stir the sauce and pilaf together and serve on a platter of baby greens, garnish with tomato wedges.

*5 Tbl. dry barley = 3/4 cup sprouted/soaked 24 hours in filtered water.

SERVES: 2

Nefertiti's Carrot Salad

A grated carrot salad accented with bell peppers and apples, tossed in a sweet sesame Pyramid Sauce.

- 1 c **Apple, cored and chopped finely**
- 1 c **Bell pepper, chopped small**
- 3 c **Carrots, finely grated (packed)**
- 1/2 c **Pyramid Sauce (page 114)**

Toss the grated carrots with the apple and bell pepper in a large bowl. Stir in 1/2 cup of *Pyramid Sauce*. Toss with your hands for an even distribution of sauce. Refrigerate.

YIELDS: 4 cups (packed)

Olive Garlic Beets

This is a zesty way to prepare beets, keep refrigerated and add to salads.

- 2 c **Beets, finely shredded (3)**
- 2-3 Tbl **Olive garlic dressing**

Toss together and refrigerate.

Oriental Barley Salad

A chewy, crunchy salad of barley, cilantro and bean sprouts in a tangy ginger marinade. This salad goes nicely with soaked sea vegetables.

	1 c	**Sprouted barley**
	1/3 c	**Cilantro, chopped, loosely packed**
	2 c	**Bean sprouts**
	1 Tbl	**Red onion, minced**
Sauce:	1 tsp	**Ginger, skinned and freshly grated**
	1/2 tsp	**Umeboshi paste**
	2 tsp	**Tamari**
	1 Tbl	**Lemon juice**

Toss together the salad ingredients in a small bowl. Stir the sauce ingredients together and fold into the salad. Marinate a few hours or overnight before serving.

SERVES: 2

Red Onion Pickles

2 c   Thinly sliced red onions
1/4 c   Lemon juice

Mix together and refrigerate overnight. Use as a condiment for sandwiches, as appetizers or serve over salads.

Spicy Sprout Salad

A nourishing truly "alive" salad of long-stemmed sprouts.
Whole sunflower seeds and buckwheat groats make great indoor greens
when soaked and planted in flats. After 7 days, they are ready to harvest.
Supermarkets and natural food stores carry pre-cut greens in produce.

3 c (packed)   Sunflower and buckwheat greens (1/4 lb combined)
1/2 Tbl   Extra virgin olive oil
2 tsp   Tamari
2½ Tbl   Lemon juice
1/4 tsp   Hot pepper sauce (or to taste)

1. Rinse and drain the sprouts and then blot dry. Cut the sprouts in half if desired.
2. Mix together the soy sauce, lemon and hot pepper sauce, and toss the mixture into the sprouts in a medium bowl. Chill.

SERVES: 2

Sunflower Sprout Salad

2 c   Sprouted sunflower seeds
3/4 c   Red cabbage, shredded
3/4 c   Green cabbage, diced
1/4 c   Cilantro leaves
1/4 c   Your favorite dressing
Cherry tomato halves as garnish

Toss everything together, chill.

Sunny Sea Salad

A very pretty salad of black hiziki (seaweed), sunflower greens and red tomato pieces.

1½ oz	Hiziki (1 pack) soak in filtered water 15 minutes, then rinse and drain.
1 c	Sunflower greens
1	Tomato, diced
1/2 c	Soaked sunflower seeds
1 Tbl	Lime juice
2 tsp	Liquid aminos
1/2 tsp	Chile sesame oil
1/2 Tbl	Brown rice vinegar

Toss and refrigerate.

SERVES: 2

Sweet Golden Salad

A golden-colored grated salad of carrots, corn and sweet potato.

2 large	Carrots, finely grated
1 ear	Sweet corn, cut off cob
1/2	Cucumber, finely shredded
1/2	Sweet potato, peeled and finely shredded
1/2	Bell pepper, chopped
1	Tomato, cut in wedges

Toss the first four ingredients together. Top with the bell pepper and tomato. Pour *Spicy Cucumber Garden Dressing* (page 116) on top, or use a dressing of your choice.

SERVES: 2

Sweet-Ziki

A sweetly seasoned hiziki salad

1¼ c	Hiziki (dried seaweed)
1 Tbl	Maple syrup
1 Tbl	Lime juice
1 tsp	Tamari

Soak the hiziki in filtered water to soften, rinse, and drain. Mix all of the ingredients together. Garnish with sesame seeds.

Thai Broccoli Salad

A terrific finely minced salad of broccoli, red pepper, cilantro and green onions, all tossed with a zesty orange-ginger-sesame Thai sauce.

	3 c	Broccoli, chopped
	1 c	Broccoli "florettes"
	1 c	Red pepper, finely chopped
	1/2 c	Green onions, minced
	1/4 c	Cilantro leaves, chopped
Sauce:	2½ Tbl	Orange juice
	1/2 tsp	Ginger, skinned and freshly grated
	1/2 tsp	Garlic, minced
	1/2 Tbl	Tamari
	2 tsp	Tahini
	1½ Tbl	Rice vinegar

1. Cut away the tough outer stalk of the broccoli stem. Chop the stems coarsely and place them in a food processor. Reserve a flew clusters for "florettes." Pulse chop to a fine mince. Transfer to a large salad bowl. Add "florettes" to bowl.
2. Pulse chop the red pepper and onions in a food processor, or cut by hand. Toss well.
3. Prepare the sauce by blending the ingredients in a blender, then toss into salad. Chill.

SERVES: 4

Tomato Corn Jubilee

A fresh salad that contrasts the sweetness of corn with the citrus tart taste of limes.

1 c	Sweet corn, cut from cob (1 ear)
1/4 c	Green onion, minced
1/4 c	Red onion, minced
2 medium	Tomatoes, seeded and chopped
1/4 c	Lime juice (2 limes)
1/2 c	Avocado, cubed
1	Garlic clove, pressed
	Freshly cracked black pepper to taste.

Put all of the ingredients into a medium bowl, toss them well. The avocado will blend in, creating a creamy sauce. Serve on chopped spinach or arugula leaves with a few sprouts on the side.

YIELDS: 2½ cups

Vibrant Pink Salad

The addition of grated beets creates a luscious pink color to this lively salad. A balanced combination of grated roots and chopped juicy vegetables.

1/4 c	Beets, chopped
3	Carrots, scrubbed
1	Yellow bell pepper, chopped
1/2	Green bell pepper, chopped
1 c	Cucumber, chopped
2	Tomatoes, seeded and chopped
2 Tbl	Onion, minced
1 recipe	*Tahiso Dressing* (page 118)

1. Grate the carrots and beets in a food processor using a fine grate blade.
2. Toss the carrots and beets into a large salad bowl along with the remaining vegetables and salad dressing.
3. Serve immediately.

Salad Dressings

Fruits and vegetables are delicious enough in their whole, "naked" state, however, we enjoy them "dressed" with various flavors for a change of taste.

*Take a broccoli to Thailand with our **Green Thai Goddess** dressing. Our **Magical Mint** dressing will take you and your favorite tomato on a journey to Egypt. Introduce the apple of your eye to the Taj Mahal in our **Curried Pumpkin** dressing. If your leafy greens seek the solace of a revitalizing spa sauce, try our no oil, fat free, **Tomato Basil** or **Orange Miso** dressings (sure to refresh any head of cabbage!).*

Wherever your traveling tastebuds may wander, our 29 delectable international "dressings" assure that your fruits and vegetables will be nattily attired.

Salad Dressings

♥ FAT FREE

Alive Salad Sauce

This is a purifying and zippy sauce.

2	Lemons, juiced
1	Garlic clove
1 Tbl	Ginger, freshly chopped
2 Tbl	Liquid aminos
1½ Tbl	Nutritional yeast
1 Tbl	Tahini
1 tsp	Barley malt syrup

Blend.

YIELDS: 1/2 cup

Avocado Sauce

Great on coleslaw and salads, but it is rich.

1 medium	Avocado
1/4 c	Cilantro leaves, packed
2	Garlic cloves
1/4 c	Lemon juice
1 Tbl	Liquid aminos
1/2 tsp	Cumin
Dash	Cayenne
1¼ c	Filtered water

Blend in blender until soft and silky.

YIELDS: 2 cups

Avomato Dressing

A creamy, spicy dressing. Omit the jalapeño if you don't want a spicy flavor.

3/4 c	Tomato juice
1/4 c	Avocado (1/2 of a small one)
2 Tbl	Lemon juice
1 small	Jalapeño, chopped
1	Garlic, pressed
2 Tbl	Filtered water

Blend in a blender. Add the water to desired consistency.

YIELDS: 1 cup

Avonana Sauce

A creamy green sauce for fruit salads.
Especially delicious over papaya or salads with banana or mango.

1 Tbl	Lime juice
1/4	Avocado
1/2	Banana
1/4 tsp	Ginger, grated
1/4 c	Filtered water

Blend in a blender.

YIELDS: 1/2 cup

Chile Peanut

*Try over a Mexican salad or in coleslaw that features
bell peppers, jicama, cabbage and carrots.*

1 c	**Tomato juice**
1 Tbl	**Peanut butter**
3/4 tsp	**Chile powder**
1 Tbl	**Lemon juice**
1	**Garlic clove**
Dash	**Cayenne**

1. Blend until smooth.
2. Tomato juice can be replaced with 3 Tbl natural ketchup, diluted with 3/4 cup of filtered water.

YIELDS: 1¼ cup

Cottage Tomato Dressing

*Similar to a "thousand island" style dressing, but better!
The seed cheese contains many beneficial enzymes which are terrific for digestion.*

1½ c	**Tomato/vegetable juice**
1/3 c	**Cottage "Seed" Cheese (page 166)**
1/2 Tbl	**White miso**
2 Tbl	**Lemon juice/lime juice**
3 Tbl	**Tahini**
1	**Garlic clove**

Blend in a blender until creamy. Or, for a chunky texture, stir in the *Cottage "Seed" Cheese* after blending the other ingredients.

YIELDS: 2 cups

Cumin Vinaigrette

Whole cumin seeds have a nutty flavor that makes this vinaigrette a special treat.

2½ Tbl	Tamari
1/3 c	Extra virgin olive oil
2 Tbl	Lemon juice
1/2 Tbl	Cumin seeds
1 or 2	Garlic cloves, pressed

Whisk all together and refrigerate in a small jar with a lid. Shake before using.

YIELDS: 2/3 cup

Curried Pumpkin Dressing

Try this on a coleslaw for an Indian flair.
This dressing tastes nice on a fruit salad, too.

4 Tbl	Lemon juice
1 c	Raw pumpkin seeds, soaked
1½ c	Filtered water
1	Garlic clove
1 Tbl	Liquid aminos
1 Tbl	Onion, chopped
2 tsp	Curry powder
1˝ piece	Fresh ginger, skinned and chopped
1 Tbl	Rice syrup or barley malt

Blend everything well.

YIELDS: 2½ cups

Curried Sunny Dulse Dressing

Dulse is a seaweed rich in protein, iron, chlorophyll, enzymes, and vitamins A and B. It contains more dietary fiber than oat bran! Try this spicy sauce with the delicious subtle flavor of dulse.

1/2 c	Sunflower seeds
1 c	Filtered water
1	Lemon, peel, seed, chop flesh
1/2 c	Dulse
1 tsp	Curry paste or powder
1/2 Tbl	Dr. Bronner's Bouillon
Dash	Cayenne
1/2 tsp	Cumin powder
1 c	Tomato juice blend
1/2	Green onion, chopped

1. After rinsing them, soak the sunflower seeds in filtered water and then cover them overnight. Strain and put them into the blender with the filtered water. Blend well. (You don't have to soak the seeds to get a good dressing, however.)
2. Peel the lemon as you would an orange, add to the blender along with the rest of the ingredients. Blend well. Sauce will thicken as it's blended.

YIELDS: 2½ cups

Ginger Cashew Sauce

Serve over Imperial Salad *(page 198) or other Asian style or seaweed salads.*

2 Tbl	Cashew butter
3 Tbl	Fresh lemon juice
1 Tbl	Soy sauce (or tamari)
1½ Tbl	Fresh ginger, skinned and chopped
1/4 tsp	Hot pepper sauce
2 tsp	Maple syrup

Blend until smooth and creamy.

YIELDS: 1 cup

Ginger Sesame Lime Sauce

A tahini sauce with a ginger accent. Serve on Sweet Potato Hiziki Pasta Salad (page 209), or any other salad with an Asian flair.

3 Tbl	Sesame tahini (raw)
1	Lime, peeled and chopped
1/2 Tbl	Ginger, freshly grated
1/2 c	Filtered water
1/2 Tbl	Mellow miso
Optional: 1 Tbl	Nutritional yeast flakes

Put everything into a blender and puree well. Refrigerate.

YIELDS: 2/3 cup

Golden Temple Dressing

Purifying and delicious!

1 c	Fresh carrot juice
1	Garlic clove
1/4 medium	Avocado
1/2	Lemon, juiced
	Small piece ginger

Blend till smooth.

YIELDS: 1¼ cups

Green Thai Goddess

Spicy and pleasing over cabbage slaws or Thai-style salads.

1½ Tbl	Peanut butter
1 Tbl	Golden miso
1 tsp	Ginger root, skinned and chopped
3/4 c	Filtered water
1/4 tsp	Red chile flakes
1/2 c	Green onions, chopped
1 tsp	Maple syrup
3 Tbl	Lime juice

Blend in a blender until creamy. Then refrigerate.

YIELDS: 1 cup

Light Cucumber Dressing

A non-fat dressing made of pureed cucumbers with dill and onion.

1 large	Cucumber, peeled, seeded, and chopped
1/4 c	Green onions, minced
1/4 c	Brown rice vinegar
1 tsp	Dill weed
1/4 c	Filtered water
1 tsp	Maple syrup
Optional: 1	Garlic clove

Blend well in a blender.

YIELDS: 1½ cups

Magical Mint Dressing

A creamy Middle Eastern-flavored dressing.
Especially great on Greek salads or tabouli.

1/4 c	Sunflower seeds (sprouted, optional)
1/2 c	Filtered water
1/2 c	Extra virgin olive oil
2 medium	Garlic cloves
1/4 c	Dried mint
1/3 c	Lemon juice
1/2 tsp	Sea salt
1 tsp	Onion powder

Put everything into a blender and "chop" for a minute. Blend on high speed another minute until smooth and creamy. Keep refrigerated.

YIELDS: 1 ½ cups

Olive Garlic Vinaigrette

A lemony vinaigrette, good on beets, or fresh chopped salads.

1/4 c	Filtered water
1/3 c	Lemon juice
1/3 c	Extra virgin olive oil
2	Garlic cloves
5	Basil leaves
1 tsp	Liquid aminos
	Cracked pepper to taste

Blend.

YIELDS: 3/4 cup

Orange Miso Dressing

Great on cabbage slaws and chilled bean salads.

1 c	Orange juice
3 Tbl	Mellow white miso
3 small	Garlic cloves
1 Tbl	Maple syrup
1 Tbl	Lemon juice

Blend till smooth.

YIELDS: 1 cup

Papaya Lime

A luscious salad sauce. Its color and texture resembles a French dressing, yet fruitier. Papayas are high in vitamin A—7,000 IU per papaya.

1 c	Ripe papaya (1/2 papaya)
2½ Tbl	Lime juice
1 tsp	Dry mustard
1/4 tsp	Cracked pepper
Pinch	Sea salt
2 Tbl	Filtered water

1. Cut the papaya in half, scoop out the seeds, peel away the skin and chop the flesh.
2. Put all of the ingredients into a blender and blend well.

SERVING SUGGESTIONS:
Serve over a butter and radicchio lettuce salad that has crumbled walnuts on top and soaked and sliced shiitake mushrooms, plus a few fresh papaya slices as a garnish.

YIELDS: 1 cup

Pesto Dressing

A nice and easy salad dressing using freshly made pesto. You also may use Besto Pesto *(page 147) or* Gingered Cashew Pesto *(page 149).*

1/4 c	**Pecan Basil Pesto (page 150)**
2 Tbl	**Filtered water**
1/2 Tbl	**Apple cider vinegar**

Blend.

YIELDS: Almost 1/2 cup

Pyramid Sauce

A sweet and spicy sauce that has a nice creamy texture from tahini.

1/3 c	**Soaked raisins**
2 Tbl	**Raw tahini**
2 Tbl	**Lemon juice**
5 Tbl	**Filtered water***
2 Tbl	**Red onion, minced**

Blend well in a blender.

*You may wish to add 1 to 2 additional tablespoons of filtered water for a thinner sauce.

YIELDS: 7/8 cup

Red Rogue Dressing

A tomato-based vinaigrette, easy to prepare and delicious.
It goes well over vegetable salads and leafy greens.

1 c	Fresh tomatoes, seeded and chopped
2 Tbl	Nutritional yeast flakes
3/4 c	Filtered water
3 Tbl	Extra virgin olive oil
1/2 tsp	Sea salt
1/2 tsp	Thyme
1/2 tsp	Dill weed
2 cloves	Garlic, chopped
1/4 tsp	Freshly cracked black pepper

Blend all of the ingredients in a blender until smooth and creamy. Keep leftovers in a bottle in the fridge.

YIELDS: 2 cups

Rose Temple Dressing

1 c	Beet juice
1	Garlic clove
1/4 medium	Avocado*
1/2	Lemon, juiced
1/2 tsp	Ginger, skinned and minced

Blend till smooth.

*Avocados are very high in fat, so use them sparingly.

YIELDS: 1 cup

Sesame Miso

*All the Asian flavors: ginger, garlic, sesame, tahini, miso and
green onion create a super salad accompaniment.*

1 c	**Filtered water**
1½ Tbl	**Mellow white miso**
1 Tbl	**Tahini**
2	**Garlic cloves, chopped**
1/2 Tbl	**Ginger, freshly chopped (skinned)**
1 Tbl	**Lemon juice**
1/2	**Green onion, chopped**

Blend in blender.

SERVING SUGGESTION:
Serve on spinach salads or sprout salads.

YIELDS: 1 cup

Spicy Cucumber Garden Dressing

*A light green cucumber sauce that is spicy from green onions,
yet creamy and thick from the seed and nut yogurt.*

1/2	**Cucumber, chopped (skinned if not organic)**
2	**Garlic cloves**
1/2 c	**Green onion, chopped**
3/4 c	**Cashew Seed Cheese Yogurt, page 165**
2 tsp	**White miso**
1/2 Tbl	**Lemon juice**
Dash	**Cayenne**

1. Pulse chop the cucumbers, garlic, and onions with the seed cheese for several seconds in a food processor.
2. Add the remaining ingredients and puree thoroughly.

YIELDS: 1¼ cups dressing

Sprouted Almond Sauce

1 c	Almonds (soaked in 2 c filtered water)
1/2 c	Filtered water
1/4 c	Lemon juice
1	Garlic clove
1 Tbl	Nutritional yeast
2 Tbl	Aminos
Dash	Cayenne and curry to taste

1. Soak the almonds overnight in filtered water to energize their vitamins and nutrients and to increase their digestibility.
2. Blend the almonds in a blender until smooth; add the remaining ingredients and blend, add filtered water if necessary.

Sprouted Sunseed Dressing

A delicious and purifying dressing.

1¼ c	Sprouted sunflower seeds
4	Garlic cloves
1/4 c	Lemon juice
2 Tbl	Aminos
1 c	Filtered water
Dash	Cayenne

1. Put all of the ingredients in a blender, adding the filtered water last; thin to desired consistency. Using the soak water from the sunseed sprouts will add more vitamins and minerals (see Sprouting Section).
2. Blend till smooth. Chill.

SERVING SUGGESTION:
Divine over vegetables or in a salad roll.

Tahiso Dressing

Oregano, garlic, and onion create savory flavors in this tahini and miso-based salad dressing. Also try as a sauce over other vegetable delights.

2 Tbl	Raw tahini
1 Tbl	Miso
1/2 c	Filtered water
1½ tsp	Oregano
1	Garlic clove, chopped
2 Tbl	Onion, minced
1 Tbl	Apple Cider Vinegar

Put all of the ingredients into a blender and blend until smooth.

Tomato Basil Salad Dressing

Bright, fresh and tasty.

1½ c	Tomatoes, chopped (4 Roma tomatoes)
1/2 tsp	Garlic, pressed
2 Tbl	Lemon juice
1/2 c	Fresh basil, loosely packed, chopped coarse

Blend in a blender for 30 seconds.

YIELDS: 1 cup (enough for a large salad for 2)

Tomato Tahini

1½ c	Tomato juice
1/2	Lemon, juiced
2	Garlic cloves
1	Jalapeño (seed first if you don't like "hot")
1½ Tbl	Tahini
1 Tbl	Nutritional yeast
1/2 Tbl	Aminos
	Cracked pepper to taste
2 Tbl	Onion, chopped

Blend all of the ingredients until smooth and creamy; adjust seasonings to taste.

Whey-Out Sauce

*A golden colored sauce prepared from using the strained liquid "whey"
that is leftover from making seed yogurts—delicious! After the yogurt has cultured
and the nut "meal" separates from the liquid "whey," use this liquid
as a base for salad dressings and sauces.*

1 c	Seed and nut "whey"*
3	Garlic cloves
1/2 c	Avocado, mashed
2 Tbl	Lemon juice
1 medium	Tomato, chopped
2 tsp	Liquid aminos
1/2 tsp	Cumin

Blend everything well in a blender.
*See the *Cultured Foods* chapter, pages 164–167.

YIELDS: 2 cups

Snackin' on the Wild Side

Yippee aye yay! These dehydrated snacks, crackers, and chips serve up something
savory and crispy without being baked, fried, or fattening.

"Whoever heard of a Live Foods cracker?" you say. Well, we did!
And it's darn good eatin', too! Made from whole sprouted grains, vegetables,
and spices, they make real nice dining companions.

This snackin' chapter also includes nouvelle sandwich rolls.
We've taken some lively spreads and combined them with herbs and spices and rolled
them in nori sushi sheets or lettuce leaves for delicious quick lunch alternatives.

Well, saddle up yer tastebuds for a little adventure,
as we take you down the Wild Side of Snackin'!

Snackin' on the Wild Side

Snacks, Crackers, and Chips

Sandwich Rolls

♥ FAT FREE

Banana Chips

A sweet and chewy treat to snack on as is, or add to fruit salads or breakfast Müesli.

4   Bananas, peeled
1/4 c   Lemon juice*

Slice the bananas 1/4˝ thick and sprinkle them with lemon juice. Place the bananas on the tray of a food dehydrator. Dry for 10 to 12 hours, until shiny on the surface yet dry to the touch.

NOTE: For an extra sweetness, dip banana in maple syrup before drying.
*The lemon juice preserves the natural banana color. You can dehydrate bananas without the lemon, however.

Banana Fingers

Use these leathery sweet treats in fruit salads, smoothies,
fruity nut milks, or for just plain snackin'.

4   Bananas, peeled

1. Push your finger through the small tip of the banana to naturally separate it into 3 sections. (You will see there is a small hole in the end where the 3 sections come together. Use your finger to coax the banana sections apart.)
2. Place the banana "fingers" on a dehydrator tray and dry for 10 to 15 hours, until leathery yet soft.

YIELDS: 12 banana "fingers"

Eggplant Pizzas

A dehydrated eggplant, tomato and seed cheese treat.

- **1 large Eggplant, peeled and sliced 1/4˝ thick**
- **1/2 c Basic Sun Almond Seed Cheese (page 165)**
- **Tomato slices 1/4˝ thick**
- **Oregano and paprika for topping.**

Put a tablespoon of the seed cheese on each eggplant disk and top with tomato slices. Place the eggplant disks in a food dehydrator for 10 hours or until dry, but still soft and pliable.

OPTIONAL: Spread miso on eggplants (1/4 tsp per large disk), then sprinkle with a sea seasoning, like Nori with ginger, or kelp and garlic.

Garden Crisps

A dehydrated whole grain cracker with savory tomato and leek.
A delicious crispy cracker to enjoy with salads or dips.

- **2 c Wheat berry sprouts**
- **1/2 c Almond pulp (from making Almond Milk)**
- **1 Tbl Sesame seeds**
- **1 Tbl Flax seeds**
- **1/2 c Leeks, chopped**
- **1½ c Tomato, chopped**
- **1 tsp Caraway seeds**
- **1 tsp Liquid aminos**

Pulse chop, then puree all of the ingredients in a food processor. Spoon out the puree onto lined dehydrator trays, then flatten into crackers. Decorate the top of the crackers with variations such as: sesame seeds, paprika, chives, or sea seasoning; or try these variations:

Mexican:	Add cumin and chile powder.
Italian:	Add basil, minced garlic and oregano.
Indian:	Add curry powder and cayenne.

Dehydrate until top of cracker is dry. Peel crackers off liners, turn them over and replace them in the dehydrator, dry until the bottom is crisp. Approximate drying time: 10 to 14 hours for bottom trays, 18 to 20 hours for top trays.

NOTE: Recipe will fill up 2½ dehydrator trays that are 12˝ in diameter.

SERVES: 4

Hawaiian Fruit Rollups

A great snack for kids of all ages.

1	Papaya, skinned and seeded
10	Strawberries
1	Banana
1/2 to 2/3 c	Pineapple juice or apple juice

Blend well in a blender. If you are using frozen strawberries, add an extra 1/4 cup of juice. Pour the blended mixture onto lined dehydrator trays and dry for 24 hours. Peel up or roll up to serve.

Party Beans

A crunchy, salty, spicy sprouted bean delight that will make your taste buds dance. Take them on a hike, sprinkle them over salads, serve them in a bowl along with your healthy drinks. Young sprouted beans dehydrate with a better taste than older sprouts. Avoid using sprouts with tails longer than 1/2˝ long.

2 c	Sprouted lentils or garbanzos*
1-2 Tbl	Tamari
Dash	Hot pepper sauce (to taste)

Mix all of the ingredients together well. Place on the mesh trays (or lined trays) of a food dehydrator. Dry for 6 to 8 hours, or until chewy-crisp.

*NOTE: You can use all combinations of pea, bean, or lentil sprouts with good results. However, the small juicy sprouts (lentils, mung) dehydrate faster and are easier to chew.

Party Peas'ers

Use freshly sprouted peas (tails no longer than 1/4") for the best taste.

1/2 c	**Whole dried green peas, sprouted (yields 2 cups)**
1 Tbl	**Tamari**
1 tsp	**Curry powder (or ginger)**

Sprout the peas until little tails appear. Shake all of the ingredients together in a plastic bag. Spread on a mesh or lined tray of a food dehydrator, dehydrate 6 hours, or until dry but not too crispy.

Savory Seeds

Use instead of croutons for a crunchy savory garnish on salads.

1/2 c	**Sprouted sunflower seeds**
1/2 tsp	**Tamari**
1/2 tsp	**Dill weed**
Dash	**Cayenne**

Stir all of the ingredients together in a small bowl. Try adding other flavorings such as 1 Tbl minced green onions, 1/2 tsp minced garlic or ginger, or 1 tsp flax seed oil.

SERVING SUGGESTION:
Sprinkle on salads as is or place in a food dehydrator till crispy.

Sprouted Herb Crackers

A simple whole grain cracker to make in your food dehydrator.

2 c	Wheatberry sprouts
1 Tbl	Kelp* (or other sea seasoning)
1/2 tsp	Basil or dill
1 tsp	Onion powder
1 tsp	Garlic powder

1. Follow the basic sprouting procedure, then put the sprouts in a food processor to grind.
2. Add the spices and pulse chop to mix together.
3. Using wet hands, shape the mixture into small walnut-sized balls. Flatten the balls between your palms and place them on a plastic-wrap lined dehydrator tray. Dehydrate for 10 hours or so, until dry. (The longer they dry, the crispier they become.)

YIELDS: 14 2½˝ wide crackers.

Sprouted Rye Crisps

This cracker has a delicious sourdough rye flavor enhanced with onion, dill and sesame. Just out of the dehydrator they are crisp and crunchy; however, they become softer after contact from the moisture in the air. For a less "sour" taste, add 1 tsp of maple syrup to the batter.

1 c	Sprouted rye berries
1 c	Sprouted wheat berries
1/2 c	Filtered water
1 Tbl	Tahini
1 Tbl	Dehydrated onion flakes
1/2 Tbl	Dill weed
1 tsp	Caraway seeds
1 tsp	Liquid aminos

1. Pulse chop the sprouts and filtered water in a food processor.
2. Add the remaining ingredients and blend together.
3. Spoon the batter onto lined dehydrator trays into 5˝ long rectangles. Top with sesame seeds, and dry 8 hours until crisp. Peel crackers off liners, turn them over, and replace them on the lined tray. Dehydrate until the bottom side is crisp.

SERVING SUGGESTIONS:
Serve with salads or soups. Top with a slice of tomato, a spread or seed cheese.

YIELDS: 10 - 12 crackers

Sprouted Wheat Thins

A delicious dehydrated cracker with mushroom, tomato and onion.

1¾ c	**Sprouted wheat berries**
1 Tbl	**Almond butter**
1/3 c	**Onion, chopped**
1/2 c	**Mushroom, chopped**
1/2 c	**Tomato, chopped**
1/2 Tbl	**Dr. Bronner's Bouillon**

Pulse chop all of the ingredients in a food processor, then blend. Spread on lined dehydrator trays and dry for 7 hours, or until crisp.

YIELDS: 10 - 12 crackers

Sprouted Wheatzas

A sprouted pizza! Assembling this is fun and you can add any toppings you like for this dehydrator "baked" delight.

1 recipe	**Sprouted Herb Crackers (page 129)**
1 recipe	**Tomato Basil Sauce (page 145)**

Other additional toppings:

> **Thinly sliced bell pepper, onions, tomatoes, or mushrooms**
> **A seed cheese of your choice**

Make the cracker dough according to the recipe. Dehydrate the dough until one side is dry to the touch, peel the cracker off the liner and place on a dehydrator tray with the moist side up. Top with the *Tomato Basil Sauce* and your favorite extra veggie toppings. Dehydrate for another 10 hours or until dry.

Sweet Potato/Yam Chips

A delicious crispy, slightly sweet chip that is made in the food dehydrator. Best eaten right from the dehydrator to retain crispness.

1   Yam or sweet potato
      Tamari
      Lemon juice

1. Peel the yam and slice it into thin sections crosswise, about 1/32 to 1/16 of an inch thick.
2. Dehydrate as is, or, spray lightly with an equal mixture of tamari, filtered water, and lemon juice.
3. Lay the chips on the food dehydrator trays to dry. Dehydrate for 10 hours or until crisp.

Yeasty Yam Chips: Follow directions above and dip in nutritional yeast after spraying with tamari mixture. Dehydrate.

Sweet Maple Yam Chips: Dip sliced roots in maple syrup seasoned with cinnamon. Dehydrate.

Veggie Pesto Rounds

These make interesting appetizers.
Try different pestos in the "spreads" section for other flavors.

1 recipe   Pecan Basil Pesto (page 150)
      1   Zucchini
4 large   Mushrooms
1 small   Eggplant

1. Slice the vegetables 1/8˝-1/4˝ thick. Spread *Pecan Basil Pesto* on top. Place on a food dehydrator tray.
2. Dry 6 to 8 hours until still a bit moist yet soft and dry to touch. You may wish to slice the vegetables paper thin for a crispy effect. Be sure to check the dryer, for thin slices dry much more rapidly than thick slices.

Zesty Potato Chips

Made in a food dehydrator, this is as close as potatoes come to being chips in a live foods diet. This recipe also can be made with turnips.

4 medium	Red potatoes, scrubbed and thinly sliced
2 Tbl	Tamari
1/2 Tbl	Garlic, pressed*
1 tsp	Lemon juice

Slice the potatoes paper thin (1/64˝-1/32˝). Stir together the tamari, garlic, and lemon and pour the mixture over the potatoes. Marinate for a couple of minutes before putting the potato chips onto the dehydrator trays. Dry 20 to 24 hours, depending on the thickness of the chips.

NOTE: Thicker slices are very hard to chew; the thinner the slice, the crispier the chip.

*You may wish to use onion powder or garlic powder instead of fresh garlic.

California Nori Roll

The classic roll—featuring avocado and sprouts.

Per roll: 1	Sushi nori sheet
3	Avocado slices
3	Tomato slices
1/3 c	Alfalfa sprouts

1. Place the avocado slices, then the tomatoes, and then the sprouts down the center of the nori sheet. Roll up the nori sheet, moistening the remaining nori edge with filtered water.
2. Continue rolling, pressing firmly to seal. You may also wish to add a dash of cayenne or seasoning on the avocado before rolling it up.

Lunafish Sushi

A delicious sushi roll filled with biogenic sprouted almonds and seasonings—an oriental ecstasy!

Per roll:
- **2 Tbl** **Lunafish Salad Spread (page 150)**
- **Tomato slices**
- **Sprouts of choice**
- **Cilantro sprigs**
- **1** **Nori (sushi) sheet**

1. Lay the *Lunafish Salad Spread* in the center of a nori sheet. Layer the tomato, sprouts, and cilantro and then roll up the nori sheet.
2. Moisten edge with water to seal. A few drops of salad dressing inside is also tasty if you like a juicy roll.
3. Slice the nori roll using a sharp, wet knife. Serve with wasabi (Japanese horseradish) and tamari as a dipping sauce if you desire.

Red Pepper Arugula Rolls

A light meal that is quick to prepare. Arugula has a wonderful nutty taste.

- **4** **Small sushi nori sheets (or cut large sheet in 1/4's)**
- **3/4 c** **Cosmic Red Pepper Salad (page 148)**
- **2** **Mushrooms, sliced**
- **24** **Arugula sprigs, washed, stems removed**
- **Optional:** **Tomato slices, red onion slices**

1. Spread 2 Tbl of the red pepper salad in the center of each nori sheet.
2. Lay 2 mushroom slices on top of the salad, then add the arugula and any of the other vegetables.
3. Roll up the nori sheet into a cone shape. Serve with a salad sauce for dipping.

SERVES: 2

Seasprout Salad Rolls

A seaweed/sprout/corn mixture deliciously tossed in a sesame dressing and stuffed inside a seaweed wrapper. Sea vegetables are rich in minerals, especially iodine, and should be a regular feature to your meals.

1/2 c	Hiziki, dried (seaweed)
1/4 c	Dulse, dried (seaweed)
1/4 c	Salad dressing*
1 c	Alfalfa sprouts (pull apart to separate)
1/4 c	Sweet white corn kernels
1/4 c	Cilantro leaves
1/2	Lime, juiced (1 Tbl)
6	Nori sheets

1. Put the hiziki and dulse into a glass bowl, pour filtered water on top of them to barely cover, stir and let sit until soft (approx. 20 minutes). Drain, rinse, drain, and set aside in a medium bowl.
2. Pour the salad dressing over the seaweeds. Toss in the sprouts, corn, cilantro, and lime.
3. Put the salad mixture in the center of each nori sheet, lengthwise, and roll up burrito style, moisten the long edge with filtered water to seal. Place on a platter. Slice nori rolls in sixths (do not fold ends in).

*Use *Sesame Miso* (page 116) or *Green Thai Goddess* (page 111) dressings for a dip.

SERVING SUGGESTION:
Garnish with sesame seeds, cucumber spears, tomato slices and cilantro sprigs.

SERVES: 6 rolls

Seed Cheese Cabbage Rolls

Peppers, pickles and carrots accent this creamy vegetable spread. Tightly rolled up in a cabbage leaf, these cabbage rolls make a perfect snack at lunch.

1¼ c	**Carrots, finely grated**
1/3 c	**Red bell pepper, minced**
1	**Garlic clove, pressed**
2/3 c	**Dream de la Cream (page 166)**
2 Tbl	**Dill pickle, minced**
1 tsp each	**Onion powder, dill weed, soy sauce**
1/4 tsp	**Grated lemon peel (optional)**
6	**Green cabbage leaves**

1. Mix the vegetables and spices into the seed cheese.
2. Using 2 heaping tablespoons of the seed cheese mixture, tightly roll up the mixture "burrito style" in a cabbage leaf. (If cabbage is tough cut out core, or use red leaf lettuce as a wrapper.)
3. Fold ends under as you roll it up to prevent the filling from escaping. Refrigerate. Makes 6 rolls.

SERVES: 2 - 3

Sprouted Sunseed Sushi

This tasty carrot/sprouted sunseed and tahini dip makes a great filling for sandwich rolls.

1/2 c	**Sprouted Sunseed Carrot Dip (page 153)**
	Sprouts
	Spinach leaves
1/2	**Tomato, sliced**
2	**Sushi nori sheets**
1/4	**Avocado, sliced**

1. Spread 1/4 cup of the dip down the center of each nori roll.
2. Lay 2 avocado slices down the center, follow with the tomato and sprouts and then pack down with the spinach leaves.
3. Roll up the nori roll tightly (moisten the edge to close). Cut in half and enjoy. Serve with *Lemon Tahini Sauce* (page 144) if desired.

YIELDS: 2 rolls

Sauces, Dips and Spreads

*Our creamy, savory and spicy Sauces, Dips, and Spreads elevate
your tastebuds to other worldly dimensions.*

*Sensational meals are yours when you serve **Creamy Pesto Sauce** or
Tomato Basil Sauce over vegetable "pasta"; stir **Cheezy Cashew Sauce** into minced
vegetables for a cosmic veggie loaf; pour **Tomato Chutney Sauce** over a "live food"
burger; stir up your universe with a **Red Chile Sauce** folded into fresh corn kernels
and chopped bell peppers creating a Santa Fe "tamale" salad.*

*Energize your day with **Awesome Guacamole** or **Lunafish Salad** atop your favorite salad,
or use any of our galaxy of spreads to fill vegetable cups, nori rolls, or lettuce leaves;
then serve them with a **Lemon Tahini Sauce** or a **Creamy Soaked Seed Sauce**.*

*Expand your taste universe with **Vegetable Seed Cheese, Pecan Basil Pesto,**
or **Besto Pesto** on a zucchini or eggplant round. Dehydrate until dry
yet soft for new flavor sensations.*

Infinite possibilities await you, there are no limitations with vibrant living foods.

Sauces

Dips and Spreads

♥ FAT FREE

Almond Ginger Sauce

Great as a dip or salad dressing, or on veggies. Highly nutritious.

1 c	**Almonds, soaked in filtered water (yields 1½ c almonds)**
2 c	**Broth (or Rejuvelac Lemonade, page 169)**
2	**Garlic cloves**
1 Tbl	**Fresh ginger, skinned and chopped**
1 Tbl	**Soy sauce**
2 Tbl	**Lemon juice**
1/8 tsp	**Cayenne (or to taste)**

Blend till smooth.

Asian Almond Sauce

A seasoned almond sauce made from enzyme rich sprouted almonds. This sauce is delicious as is, and is made even better by culturing on your counter. Culturing bestows your seed sauces with airborne lactobacillus, great for intestinal flora.

1 c	**Sprouted almonds**
1 c	**Filtered water**
1/4 c	**Rejuvelac Lemonade (page 169)***
1 Tbl	**Raw tahini**
1	**Garlic clove**
1/2 tsp	**Grated fresh ginger**

Blend all of the above ingredients in a blender for a couple of minutes. Enjoy now, or pour sauce into a large glass jar (large enough to hold 2¼ cups). Cover the top of the jar with a towel and let sauce ferment for 8 hours on the counter. Stir together and spoon over vegetable creations.

*You may substitute filtered water, but add 2 teaspoons of miso paste to encourage fermentation.

Cheezy Cashew Sauce

A thick and creamy savory sauce that can be added to minced vegetables, poured over a salad, or used as a dip.

3/4 c	**Cashew pieces (soak in filtered water overnight, drain)**
1 c	**Filtered water**
1 tsp	**Sea salt**
1 tsp	**Garlic powder**
2 tsp	**Onion powder**
3 Tbl	**Nutritional yeast flakes**
2 Tbl	**Lemon juice**
1/4 c	**Rolled oats**

Put all of the ingredients into a blender and blend on "chop" to break up cashews. Blend on high speed for 3 minutes (or more) until creamy. The long high speed blending warms up the cheezy sauce.

YIELDS: 1 cup

Cilantro Cashew Sauce

A luscious creamy green sauce with oriental flavors.

1/2 c	**Cilantro leaves, chopped**
1/2 c	**Soaked cashews**
1/2 Tbl	**Ginger, skinned and minced**
1 Tbl	**Garlic, chopped**
3 Tbl	**Filtered water (or to thin)**
1/2 tsp each	**Umeboshi paste and miso**
Optional: 1 tsp	**Serrano chile, seeded and minced**

Blend in a blender until smooth.

Creamy Pesto Sauce

Delicious over salads and stuffed veggies. Tastes like pesto.

3/4 c	**Cashew Seed Cheese Yogurt (page 165)**
1/2 c	**Basil leaves**
2	**Garlic cloves, pressed**
1 Tbl	**Extra-virgin olive oil (optional)**
1/4 c	**Filtered water (or Rejuvelac Lemonade)**
2 Tbl	**Lemon juice**
1 tsp	**Liquid aminos**

Thin seed yogurt down with *Rejuvelac Lemonade* (page 169) or "whey" (left over liquid from making seed yogurt) to a light batter consistency.

Blend, add filtered water as desired.

YIELDS: 1¼ cups

Creamy Soaked Seed Sauce

A yummy basic seed and nut sauce.
Mild enough to go with fruits or vegetable salads.

1/4 c	**Almonds, soaked in filtered water**
1/4 c	**Sun seeds, sprouted**
1½ c	**Filtered water**
1/2	**Date, soaked**
1/2	**Lemon, juiced**
1 tsp	**White miso**

Blend, add filtered water to the desired consistency.

YIELDS: 2 cups

Lemon Tahini Sauce

A lovely lemon colored sauce to serve on salads and other delights.

1/2 c	Tahini
1	Whole lemon, peeled, seeded and chopped
1	Garlic clove
1½ c	Filtered water
1½ Tbl	White miso paste
1 tsp	Hot pepper sesame oil (optional)
1/2 tsp	Turmeric powder (optional, to increase yellow color)

Blend everything in a blender until creamy smooth. Adding tumeric will slightly alter the flavor and provide a nice yellow gold color.

YIELDS: 2½ cups

Peanut Sauce

A savory sauce for dipping vegetables, or serve with a dehydrated veggie burger.

2 Tbl	Peanut butter
2 Tbl	Lemon juice
1 Tbl	White miso
1	Garlic clove
2	Green onions, chopped
2 Tbl	Nutritional yeast flakes
1/4 c	Filtered water
1/2 tsp	Curry powder

Blend well in a blender.

YIELDS: 3/4 cup

Red Chile Sauce

A delicious "enchilada style" sauce. Toss with sprouted beans and vegetables, or use on top of a salad.

2	**Tomatoes, seeded and chopped**
1	**Serrano chile, sliced**
1	**Lime, juiced**
1 Tbl	**Red chile powder (not cayenne!)**
1/2 Tbl	**Cumin powder**
1 large	**Garlic clove, chopped**
1 tsp each	**Basil, oregano, and liquid aminos**

Blend in a blender.   YIELDS: 1 cup

Tomato Basil Sauce

A wonderful fresh marinara sauce.
Organically grown tomatoes need little else for a delicious sauce.

3 c	**Tomatoes, peeled and seeded, (3-4 large)**
1/2 c packed	**Basil leaves, chopped**
2	**Garlic cloves, pressed**

1. To easily peel tomatoes: Place tomatoes in a large bowl, pour near boiling filtered water over them and cover the bowl for 5 to 10 minutes. Peel, seed, and chop.
2. Pulse chop the basil and garlic in a food processor. Add the chopped tomatoes to the food processor and pulse down 5 quick times until just mixed. (Do not puree!)
3. Pour over vegetable "pasta" or serve with dehydrated grain burgers or "pizza."

YIELDS: 3 cups. Serves 2 sauce lovers.

Tomato Chutney Sauce

This sweet and spicy chutney makes a great dip and is a nice change of pace for a salad dressing.

3 medium	**Tomatoes, skin and seed**
3 Tbl	**Raisins**
1 tsp	**White miso**
1 tsp	**Serrano chile, chopped (use to taste)**
4 tsp	**Lemon juice**
2 tsp	**Ginger root, skinned and minced**

Blend in a blender. Add an additional chopped tomato for texture.

YIELDS: About 2 cups

Dips and Spreads

Also see the Cultured Foods chapter for sensational seed cheese recipes which make wonderful spreads.

Almond Bean Paté

This is a "sprouted" mung bean paté.
Use to stuff mushrooms, as a dip, or accompaniment to salads.

2 Tbl	Almond butter
3/4 c	Mung bean sprouts
1/4 c	Green onions, chopped
1 Tbl	Cilantro leaves, chopped
2	Garlic cloves, pressed
Dash	Cayenne
1/2 Tbl	Lemon juice
1/4 c	Almonds, sprouted
1 tsp	Minced lemon peel
1/4 tsp	Thyme

Blend in a food processor.

YIELDS: About 1¼ cups

Awesome Guacamole

The classic avocado dip; creamy, zesty, and yes—fattening!
Use for a topping to salads or dip for veggies.

2 medium	Avocados, mashed
2 tsp	Jalapeños, minced
1/2 c	Tomato, seed and chop
1 Tbl	Lime juice
1 tsp	Garlic, minced
1 Tbl	Red onion, minced
2 Tbl	Cilantro, minced
	Cracked pepper and sea salt to taste
Garnish: 1 Tbl	Green onion, minced

Mash avocadoes with a fork in a small bowl. Stir in the remaining ingredients. To prevent avocadoes from discoloring, place the avocado pit on top before storing.

SERVES: 4 - 6 (1½ cups)

Besto Pesto

A fresh pesto that is delicious as a dip, as a stuffing for mushroom caps
or celery ribs, or as a spread on crackers.

1/3 c	Pine nuts
1 Tbl	Garlic, chopped
1/3 c	Fresh cilantro, packed leaves, chopped
1/3 c	Fresh basil, packed leaves, chopped
1 Tbl	Lemon juice
1 c	Tomato, chopped
1/2 tsp	Sea salt

Put all of the ingredients into a food processor, except the tomatoes, and pulse chop several times. Stop to scrape down the sides and repeat. Add the tomatoes and continue to pulse chop until just blended. Keep a texture to the pesto, it should not be a puree. Chill or serve.

Cosmic Red Pepper Spread

*Red peppers create a lovely soft pink color to this exciting spread.
Sprouted sunseeds, creamy cashews, lemon, dill, and kelp combine
to yield a high-powered, delicious mock salmon.*

1 c	Red pepper, chopped
1 c	Sprouted sunflower seeds
2 Tbl	Red onion, chopped
2 Tbl	Lemon juice, with 1/2 tsp grated rind
2 tsp	Kelp seasoning
1/2 c	Cashew pieces, finely ground
1 tsp	Dill weed
1/2 Tbl	White miso
	Cracked pepper to taste

Pulse chop the red peppers in a food processor, then add the remaining ingredients and puree. Refrigerate.

SERVING SUGGESTIONS:
Spread on Garden Crisps (page 126), use to top a salad, use as a filling in peppers, tomato halves, celery sticks, or Nori sushi rolls.

YIELDS: About 2 cups

Elephant Spread

1	Banana, ripe
1 Tbl	Peanut butter (substitute 2 Tbl. grated apple for a non-fat version)

Mix together and spread on celery sticks or apple slices. Sprinkle raisins on top.

SERVES: 2 - 3

Gingered Cashew Pesto

Wow! Tastes like butter, but better. A creamy green pesto with a ginger kick.

1 c	Cilantro leaves
1/2 c	Raw cashews
3 Tbl	Lime juice
1/4 c	Extra virgin olive oil
1 Tbl	Garlic, chopped
2 tsp	Ginger root, peeled and chopped
	Cayenne and sea salt to taste

Puree all of the ingredients in a food processor using a pulse chop motion. Scrape down the sides once while making. Put into a small bowl. Refrigerate.

Greek Olive Pesto

Spicy, thick, and rich. Use sparingly as a spread on dehydrated crackers or eggplant slices. Kalamata olives are the small, dark purple ones with an oily outside.

1/2 c	Sprouted sun seeds
16	Black Kalamata olives, pitted
1/4 c	Basil leaves
1	Serrano chile, minced
2 - 3 Tbl	Filtered water or lemon juice

Grind in a food processor or blender until smooth. Refrigerate.

Lunafish Salad Spread

A yummy dip or a salad stuffing.
Serve in celery ribs, on bell pepper wedges, or to top a salad.

1 c	Carrots, finely grated (approx. 3-4 carrots)
3	Celery stalks, minced
3 Tbl	Lemon juice
1 c	Sprouted almonds
1/2 Tbl	Liquid aminos or quick sip
1/2 Tbl	Kelp or nori sea seasoning
1/2 c	Green onions, chopped

1. Finely grate the carrots in a food processor, then transfer to a measuring cup.
2. Place chop blade in the processor, then put the remaining ingredients in and pulse chop. Scrape down the sides, then continue to pulse chop into a paste for a couple of minutes. Refrigerate.

SERVING SUGGESTION
Use this spread in Lunafish Sushi, *page 133.*

Pecan Basil Pesto

A fragrant pesto with a nice garlic and lemon lift.
Spread it on eggplant, mushrooms, or zucchini rounds.
For a special treat, dehydrate these into "Veggie Pesto Rounds" (page 131).

1½ c	Basil leaves
1/3 c	Pecans, finely ground
1 Tbl	Garlic, chopped
2 - 3 Tbl	Lemon/lime juice
Pinch	Sea salt

Rinse and tear the basil leaves in half. Put all of the ingredients into a blender and grind. You may need to stop and stir a couple of times during blending. Refrigerate.

Pineapple Salsa

A delightful tropical salsa. Serve with Mexican dishes, or toss 1/4 cup of this salsa into 2 cups of papaya chunks for a deliciously different salad.

2 c	**Pineapple chunks**
1/2 c	**Onion, minced**
1/4 c	**Cilantro leaves**
1/2	**Lemon, juiced**
2	**Jalapeños, seeded**
1	**Garlic clove, pressed**
1 tsp	**Crumbled oregano**

1. Press the garlic and 1 jalapeño through a garlic press, thinly slice the second jalapeño.
2. Put all of the ingredients into a medium bowl and toss.

SERVING SUGGESTIONS:
Serve with Spicy Chile Beans *(page 207) or* Black Bean Fiesta Salad *(page 191).*

Salsa Fresca

Serve with sprouted crackers or dehydrated chips, or as a condiment with all sorts of foods.

9 - 12	**Tomatoes, seed and chop**
1/2	**Red onion, finely chop**
1/2	**Yellow onion, finely chop**
4	**Jalapeños, seed and mince**
1 c	**Cilantro leaves, loosely packed**
2 Tbl	**Apple cidar vinegar**
4	**Garlic cloves, pressed**
1/2 tsp	**Sea salt (optional)**
1/2 tsp	**Cumin powder**

Put all of the ingredients into a medium bowl and stir. Keep refrigerated.

Spicy Peanut Spread

Dynamically delicious! Use on sprouted crackers or vegetables.
Thin with a bit of filtered water for a sauce.

1 c	Raw peanuts (unsalted)
2 Tbl	Ginger, skinned and freshly chopped
1 Tbl	Garlic, chopped
1/2 c	Onion, chopped
1/2 c	Peeled tomatoes, chopped
1/3 c	Fresh cilantro leaves, packed
1/4 c	Lime or lemon juice
1 Tbl each	Tamari and natural ketchup
1 tsp each	Cumin and chile powder
	Cayenne to taste

1. Pulse chop the peanuts, ginger, garlic, and onion in a food processor. Stop and scrape down the sides.
2. Add the remaining ingredients and puree.

Spicy Sesame Gomasio

A savory accompaniment to serve on top of salads or as a garnish on sauces or soups. Gomasio is a spice blend using whole or ground sesame seeds. This one is loaded with both the Essential Fatty Acids found within flax seeds.

1/2 c	Flax seeds
1/4 c	Sesame seeds
1/4 c	Pumpkin seeds
1 Tbl	Onion powder
2 tsp	Chile powder blend
1/8 tsp	Sea salt
Dash	Cayenne

1. Grind the seeds in a grinder or mill, then add the remaining ingredients to the bowl and toss well.
2. Store in an airtight container and chill.

NOTE: You can use walnuts, sunflower seeds, nori, dulse, and nutritional yeast for other gomasio combinations. Experiment! Enjoy it on salads and other dishes.

Sprouted Lentil Spread

*Spread on celery stalks, use as a stuffing for lettuce leaves,
or in red pepper sections, or use to top a salad.*

1 c	Celery, minced
1½ Tbl	White miso
1 Tbl each	Garlic and ginger, skinned and freshly minced
2 c	Sprouted lentils
5 Tbl	Nutritional yeast flakes
1/2 c	Cashews, finely ground
1/2 tsp	Cumin
1 tsp	Basil
	Cayenne to taste
2 Tbl	Tahini

Add to a food processor in the order given and grind well. Refrigerate.

YIELDS: 2 cups

Sprouted Sunseed Carrot Dip

*A nourishing stuffing from sprouted sunflower seeds,
grated carrots, ginger and spices. This delightful sandwich stuffing
can be whipped up in your food processor in a few minutes.*

1½ c	Carrots, finely grated
1¼ c	Sunflower seeds, sprouted 2-3 days
1/4 c	Red onion, chopped
4 tsp	Lemon juice
2 Tbl	Tahini
2½ tsp	White miso
2 tsp	Ginger root, skinned and minced
1	Garlic clove
1/4 c	Filtered water
1/4 tsp	Serrano pepper, minced

1. Finely grate the carrots in a food processor. Transfer to a bowl.
2. Put the remaining items into the food processor and pulse chop until blended. Scrape sides as needed.
3. Add the carrots, and pulse chop to a puree. Chill. Use as a filling in nori sheets, lettuce leaf sandwiches, sandwiches, or as a dip.

Sunshew Spread

A delicious vegan "chopped liver" spread. Packed with protein and vitamins.

1/4 c	Sunflower seeds, soaked overnight in filtered water
1/4 c	Cashew pieces, soaked overnight in filtered water
1 tsp	Ginger, skinned and freshly grated
1	Garlic clove, pressed
1 tsp	Lemon juice
2/3 c	Lentil sprouts
1/4 c	Red onion, chopped
2 tsp	Curry powder
1 tsp	Cumin powder

1. Strain the water from the soaked seeds and nuts. Put the nuts and seeds into a food processor and pulse chop.
2. Add the remaining ingredients and continue to blend until a thick paste forms. Store in fridge.

YIELDS: About 1 cup

Vegetable Seed Cheese

Mix seed cheese with the pulp from making vegetable juices. A healthy combo.

1/2 c	Basic Sun Almond Seed Cheese (page 165)
1/2 c	Carrot or beet pulp
1 tsp each	Lemon juice, liquid aminos
1 tsp each	Ginger and garlic, skinned and minced

Stir together. Use as a sandwich filling, on crackers or in sushi rolls—enzyme packed!

Yalmond Cheese Stuffing

A delicious stuffing of grated yams and fermented almond yogurt, resembling a mock salmon spread. Easy to make and very high in enzymes and vitamins. Put stuffing in a half of a pepper or a tomato for a fine meal.

1 c	**Seasoned Nut Cheeses and Yogurts (fermented 6 hours) (page 167)**
1	**Jewel yam, peel and finely grate**
1	**Garlic clove**
1/4 c	**Cashews or almonds, ground***
2 Tbl	**Fresh dill**

Mix all of the ingredients together in a medium bowl. Use to stuff peppers, tomatoes, or celery—yummy! Feel free to substitute grated beets or carrots for the yam.

*NOTE: If your seed cheese is firm, omit added nuts.

YIELDS: Enough to fill 3 medium bell peppers (6 halves)

Cultured Foods

*"Cheeses" from seeds and "Wines" from wheat? These cultured foods
don't necessarily have more "class," but they do have culture!*

*Your kitchen will become alive with culinary alchemy and you'll
have fun exploring the world of fermentation.*

*Entice yourself with vegetables fermented with herbs and spices!
Experience **Curried Carrot Kraut** for a downright delicacy or **Classic Dilly Kraut**
for a traditional tasting kraut. These easy to prepare sauerkrauts are loaded with flavor,
and are full of plant enzymes and lactic acid for healthy digestion.*

*You will discover a symphony of new tastes in our classic seed cheese:
Basic Sun Almond Seed Cheese, which provides a versatile cultured food
that can be turned into a firm "cheese," or added to salad
dressings, sauces, or vegetables to create salad loaves.*

*Experience our **Cottage "Seed" Cheese** which has a creamy, chunky
texture like cottage cheese. Transform your meals with our **Dream de la Cream**, a silky
smooth spread similar to cream cheese made from cashews and macadamia nuts.*

*Besides these cultured nut and seed ecstasies, you will quench
your thirst with cultured wheat beverages called biogenic drinks. Biogenic
because they are cultured from actively alive sprouted wheat, which is filled with much
regenerative energy. Try **Rejuvelac Lemonade**, a powerful cellular cleanser which is
the cultured water from "sprouted" (actively alive) wheat berries.
Blending wheat sprouts with a bit of maple syrup or dried fruit,
Rejuvelac Lemonade is transformed into a wheat "wine,"
which we call **Sprouted Wheat Divine**.*

A cultured palate is filled with the tastes of life!

Cultured Foods

Live Sauerkraut

Seed and Nut Yogurts and Cheeses

Biogenic Drinks—Liquid Heroes

♥ FAT FREE

Live Sauerkraut

It really is quite easy making your own delicious health building sauerkraut. Sauerkraut (soured vegetable) is a fermented food rich in lactic acid and digestive enzymes. Lactic acid feeds the beneficial bacteria (lactobacillus acidophilus) in your intestines. These beneficial bacteria assist in detoxifying your body. Lactic acid is necessary for the vitality and growth of new cells. Sauerkraut assists in your cleansing and detoxification process and contributes to your overall health.

There is no need for salt in live sauerkraut. Our sauerkrauts are 100% pure stuff! You can use combinations of hard fibrous vegetables in your krauts: celery, cauliflower, beets, cabbage (red and green), daikon, and even broccoli. Flavor your krauts with any spice or spice combos you like: ginger, dulse, garlic, onion, dill, basil, or curry. One or two herbs will create a full-flavored kraut.

Classic Dilly Kraut

*Hints of dill, garlic and onion accent green cabbage nicely. You may add
2 teaspoons of pulverized celery seed or caraway to add extra flavor.*

1 large firm	**Green cabbage, chopped**
1/2 large	**Red onion, chopped**
2	**Garlic cloves, pressed**
1½ Tbl	**Dill weed**

1. Wash and clean the vegetables. Remove the few outer leaves of cabbage and set them aside. (These will be used to cover the sauerkraut.)
2. Grate the vegetables in a food processor. The juicier you can make them the better, since the juice is the medium which activates the fermentation.
3. Toss all of the vegetables and spices into a large bowl, then transfer them to a stainless steel, glass, or earthen crock. Pack the vegetables down using your hands, so you get all the air out. The juice should come up between your fingers. If it doesn't, create more juice by either (a) Blending 2 cups of grated cabbage with 1 cup of filtered water, or (b) Juicing 1 to 2 cups of grated cabbage. Then, add this to your vegetables.
4. Cover the grated vegetables with the outer leaves of the cabbage, pressing down hard. Find a plate that fits just inside of your crock and press it down over the cabbage leaves.
5. Weight down the plate with a bowl or jar filled with water—the heavier the better. Cover this assemblage with a kitchen towel and let it rest for 4 to 7 days on your counter at room temperature. (70° to 80°F is ideal).
6. Taste test your kraut for a zingy flavor after day 4 if the weather is warm. Sauerkraut will take longer to ferment in cold weather. Remove the outer cabbage leaves and any discolored area on the surface of your kraut. If it has that "zing," and is tasty, it is ready. Refrigerate the kraut once it is ready in sealed glass containers to prevent further fermentation. If stored in this fashion, your kraut will keep for several months.

YIELDS: 9 cups of kraut

Curried Carrot Kraut

*A sensational kraut! The carrots provide a bit of sweetness
which compliments the curry, as well as contributing to a lovely orange color.
A delicious full-flavored kraut, great as a side dish or over a salad.*

1	Green cabbage, chopped
6 medium to large	Carrots, chopped
1 small	Red onion, chopped
1½-2 Tbl	Curry powder
1	Garlic clove, pressed

Follow directions for our *Classic Dilly Kraut* recipe (page 162). To create extra juiciness, juice 2 of the carrots and stir the juice into the remaining ingredients.

Ruby Ginger Kraut

*This ruby-colored sauerkraut has a gentle sweet taste
from the apple and ginger—a sublime zing!*

1 medium	Red cabbage, grated coarse
3 medium	Beets, grated fine
9 ribs	Celery, sliced thin
1 c	Apple juice (press it fresh from 4 Gala apples!)
2½ Tbl	Ginger, juiced
1/3 c	Filtered water

Mix all of the above ingredients together in a large bowl. Proceed with instructions under *Classic Dilly Kraut* (page 162).

Maximize Your Digestive Health with Seed and Nut "Cheeses" and "Yogurts"!

We refer to our cultured seed and nut products as "Cheeses" and "Yogurts," even though they are all plant based and are not derived from any dairy or animal products.

The "cheeses" have been created from a mixture of (soaked) nuts or seeds blended with filtered water, which is then allowed to culture for 8 to 10 hours in a warm draft-free environment. The "whey," or liquid, separates to the bottom of the jar and the "cheese" floats to the top giving off a delicious ripe lemon-like aroma. The "cheese" is then ready to be scooped out and enjoyed, or if it's allowed to drain through a cheesecloth for 4 hours or more, it will yield a firmer "cheese."

The "yogurts" are made using the same process, however, before the "whey" actually begins to separate out, the yogurt is ready (about 4 to 6 hours).

Use this delicious "whey" to make salad dressings and sauces.

Include these live "cheeses" and "yogurts" in your diet to provide your body with the beneficial plant enzymes which are made available through the fermentation process. Culturing seed and nut sauces makes them easy to digest, because the fermentation process predigests the protein, fats, and carbohydrates present in the raw seeds and nuts. The result is a biogenic food that is loaded with plant enzymes and airborne lactobacillus cultures which are beneficial to digestion and enrich the entire body's cellular physiology.

Use them to enrich a salad, to bind together grated raw vegetables, to top a fruit salad, or to put into a salad dressing or sauce. They combine well with any food.

Enjoy these recipes in good health, and may you have as much fun creating them as we do!

Basic Sun Almond Seed Cheese

A delicious yogurt-style "cheese" made from cultured nuts and seeds.
Use it in salad dressings or on top of a salad; flavor it with
herbs, garlic, or spices for sauces and dips.

1/2 c	**Raw sunflower seeds**
1 c	**Raw almonds**
2 c	**Filtered water (or Rejuvelac Lemonade, page 169)**
1 tsp	**White miso**

1. Finely grind the nuts and seeds in a food mill until powdery fine. Transfer them to a blender.
2. Blend one cup of filtered water with the nut powder, then add the remaining ingredients and blend well.
3. Pour your seed yogurt into a jar, put a kitchen towel on top and let your "seed yogurt" ferment for 8 hours, minimum, yielding a delicious product. You can let it ferment for 20 hours if you like a nice "sour" yogurt-style flavor.
4. Spoon "cheese" off of the top and save "whey" (liquid at bottom) for salad dressings such as *Whey-Out Sauce*, page 119. At this point the soft nut cheese is ready to use. To create a firmer cheese, put this mixture into a cheesecloth and tightly secure the top. Let it drain over a bowl overnight until desired firmness is achieved. Season to taste.

*MORE EXCITING RECIPE VARIATIONS USING THIS **BASIC SUN ALMOND SEED CHEESE** ARE FOUND ON THE "QUICK MEAL IDEAS," PAGE 247.

Cashew Seed Cheese Yogurt

A creamy, richer tasting yogurt using cashews.
The Rejuvelac Lemonade quickens the culturing process.

1/4 c	**Sesame seeds**
1/2 c	**Sunflower seeds**
1/2 c	**Cashews**
1¼ c	**Rejuvelac Lemonade (page 160)**
1 tsp	**White miso**

Follow the directions for *Basic Sun Almond Seed Yogurt* (page 165).

Cottage "Seed" Cheese

A vegan specialty. Use like cottage cheese.
It's chunky texture compliments both fruit and vegetable salads,
and it also makes a nice stuffing or filling. Season to taste for a variety of flavors.

1 c	**Raw almonds**
1/2 c	**Cashew pieces**
1/2 c	**Sunflower seeds**
1 c	**Filtered water or Rejuvelac Lemonade (page 169)**
Optional: 1/4 c	**Raw macadamia nuts**

1. Put the nuts and seeds in a large bowl and cover with filtered water. Soak overnight.
2. Strain away the water, then rinse away the oils which float to the surface. Put the soaked nuts and seeds into a blender with filtered water and blend partially (not creamy smooth). Leaving the texture chunky gives it the resemblance to cottage cheese.
3. Pour the mixture into a glass jar with a wide opening, put a kitchen towel on top of the jar, and let the cheese sit to culture for 10 hours, until bubbles appear. Refrigerate after it has cultured.

YIELDS: 3 cups

Dream de la Cream

A fermented seed "cream" that is out of this world! So delicious and creamy, it makes a great spread on bread or crackers or with a salad. This cheese uses finely ground raw nuts (not soaked), then they get "cultured" or fermented in Rejuvelac.

1/3 c	**Raw macadamia nuts**
2/3 c	**Cashews**
1/2 c	**Almonds**
1 c	**Filtered water or Rejuvelac Lemonade (page 169)**

Finely grind the nuts in batches in a nut grinder. Put the nut powder into a blender with one cup of filtered water or *Rejuvelac Lemonade,* blend, add the remaining liquid, blend again and pour into a glass jar. Cover with a kitchen towel and let it sit to "culture" for 8 to 12 hours. Spoon out and enjoy.

YIELDS: 2 cups (a rich treat, so use sparingly)

Seasoned Nut Cheeses

Your cultured seed and nut products can be enhanced by this basic recipe. Feel free, however, to substitute fresh ginger or herbs to create different international flavorings. This savory blend is our favorite.

1 c	**Almonds (soaked)**
1 Tbl	**Peanut butter**
1 Tbl	**Golden miso**
1/4 c	**Onion, chopped**
1	**Garlic clove, chopped**
2 tsp	**Umeboshi (plum) paste**
Optional: 1/2 Tbl	**Herbs (oregano, cumin, basil, dill, etc.)**

1. Strain the almonds and put them into a blender along with the remaining ingredients. Add 2 cups of filtered water and puree them together.
2. Pour the puree into a glass jar and culture for 6 to 10 hours or until separation occurs. Spoon out and enjoy!

Sprouted Sunflower Seed Cheese

Instead of using raw seeds as in Basic Sun Almond Seed Cheese, *this recipe uses sprouted sunflower seeds, the leanest of the seeds. Culturing a sprouted seed heightens the biogenic properties, making it a strong tasting seed cheese.*

1/2 c	**Soaked cashews**
1½ c	**Sunflower seeds, sprouted 1 or 2 days**
1 c	**Filtered water**
1 tsp	**White miso**

Blend all the ingredients in a blender, pour the blended mixture into a glass jar, loosely cover with a towel and let it sit for 6 to 8 hours, so fermentation can occur. For a firm cheese, spoon fermented "cheese" mixture into cheesecloth, twist ends together on top, and hang the fermented "cheese" in the cheesecloth over a bowl for 6 to 8 hours until it is firm.

WHAT TO DO WITH THE "WHEY"?

Never throw this liquid a-whey! It is rich in nutrients and will make a delicious salad dressing. Follow this guideline for a savory salad sauce.

1/2 c seed and nut "whey", 1 Tbl apple cider vinegar, 1/2 tsp curry powder, 1 tsp dill weed, 1 garlic clove, pressed, and 1 tsp liquid aminos or miso.

Stir together or blend. Add more cider vinegar to taste.

Rejuvelac Lemonade
Our basic Health Cocktail

Who would've guessed that sprouted wheat berries and filtered water could be the catalysts for fermentation (fermentation is controlled aging—certain temperatures and times of maturation are essential to obtain the desired results or cultures), yielding a wonderful rejuvenating drink loaded with B vitamins, live enzymes, protein and minerals. It is good for you and good to drink with your meals (one of the few liquids that won't interfere with digesting food). In fact, Rejuvelac Lemonade *contains friendly lactic acid bacteria, the kind found in yogurt.*

> 1/2 c   **Sprouted wheat berries (soaked 24 hours and sprouted 2 days)**
> 6 c   **Filtered water**

1. Put the fresh sprouted wheat berries and one cup of the filtered water into a blender. Blend on "chop" to break up the sprouts. Add one more cup of filtered water and then blend again.
2. Pour the blended mixture into a large glass jar, add the remaining water and cover with a kitchen towel. Stir twice daily to activate the mixture which helps to improve the taste. It will take three days before it is ready. It will have a tart lemon-like taste with a characteristic sauerkraut-like aroma-flavor. If it smells bad or does not have a tart lemon-like taste, discard it and start over. Spoiled Rejuvelac may have unfriendly bacteria rather than friendly bacteria, do **not** drink it.
3. Enjoy this "alive" drink one cup a day to start. As your body becomes accustomed to its cleansing effects, increase your daily quantity as desired.
4. Strain the Rejuvelac mixture into a jar and store it in the fridge. (It will last about two weeks.) Refill the first starter batch with more filtered water, and cultivate another batch. This will only take two days, and won't be as strong, but will still taste delightful and refreshing.

Mango Bango

A creamy tropical cooler with the live enzyme benefits of rejuvelac. This drink is a rejuvelac smoothie.

3/4 c	Frozen mango chunks
1 c	Rejuvelac Lemonade, page 168
2 Tbl	Lime juice
1 Tbl	Maple syrup

Blend all of the ingredients well in a blender. Serve the mixture on ice with a lime twist.

SERVES: 2

Rejuvenating Lemonade

A delightful lemon/lime aide boosted with a hint of pineapple, enchanting to the palate. When blended, it has a thick frothy head. Our favorite!

1/2 c	Lemon/lime juice
1½ c	Rejuvelac Lemonade, page 168
1/4 c	Pineapple juice
1/4 c	Pure maple syrup
1 c	Ice cubes

Blend all of the ingredients in a blender until they are frothy. Serve the mixture over ice cubes with a lemon or lime slice and a pineapple wedge.

SERVES: 3

Pineapple Rejuvenator

A healthy and refreshing drink. Good for digestion and for promoting intestinal flora.

4 oz	Pineapple juice, chilled
4 oz	Rejuvelac Lemonade (see above)

Stir together in a glass.

SERVES: 1

Spirit of Sauerkraut

This enzyme-rich drink soothes the digestive tract and promotes healthy intestinal flora. An abundant supply of friendly bacteria is found in both the Rejuvelac and sauerkraut. Toast to your good health!

1 c	Rejuvelac Lemonade, page 168
1/4 c	Sauerkraut, naturally fermented

Blend well in a blender. Serve in champagne flutes.

SERVES: 1

Rejuvelac Sprouted Wheat Divine

Follow the basic Rejuvelac Lemonade procedure on page 168, then add raisins, or other dried fruit for different sweet flavors. Adding herbs and extracts creates various "wines," while adding beets makes our "rosé" variety. Enjoy these fresh zippy cocktails as we salute your health!

Basic Recipe

1. Pulse chop 3/4 cup raisins in a blender when making Step 1 of *Rejuvelac Lemonade* (page 169).
2. Proceed with the rest of Steps 2 and 3, straining out the raisins before serving. The raisins provide the natural sugar to assist in the process of fermentation.

Elixir de Apricot

A delicate golden apricot health beverage.

2 c	**Rejuvelac Sprouted Wheat Divine (above)**
1/4 c	**Soaked apricots, chopped**
1 Tbl	**Maple syrup or frozen pineapple concentrate**
1/4 tsp	**Vanilla extract**

Blend everything in a blender for one minute and strain into a glass jar. Serve chilled.

Divine Rosé

3 c	**Rejuvelac Sprouted Wheat Divine (above)**
1½ Tbl	**Beets, minced**
1 Tbl	**Maple syrup**
1/4 c	**Currants**

Blend everything in a blender for one minute. Strain liquid and refrigerate.

The Enchanted Tureen

*Venture into our blended creations of vibrant and alive soups!
These juicy soups are loaded with plant enzymes, vitamins, minerals, and vitality in
every dynamic spoonful. Your imagination will soar to new heights as our easy to
prepare vibrant soups enchant you with their fresh, fabulous flavors.*

*__Chilled Papaya Mint Bisque, Cucumber Soup,__ and __Alfalfa Fennel Soup__ are appetite
enticers which are meant to be served before a meal or in between courses. They have
light and cleansing effects on the palate and are refreshing additions to a meal.*

*Try __Borscht, Gazpacho,__ or __Almond Corn Wowder__ with a salad
for a wonder-filled lunch or a "light" dinner.*

*__Hearty Lentil, Sprouty-Strone, Garden Ginger Energy Soup,__ and __Euphoria Soup__ are
main course soups loaded with minced vegetables or sprouted legumes.*

*Blend all your soups with love and you will transform
the soup du jour into soup du coeur!*

The Enchanted Tureen

Fruit Soups

Vegetable Soups

♥ FAT FREE

Apple Pear Bisque

A creamy fruit soup with a slight lemon tang.
This makes a refreshing first course, or a light lunch.

2	**Pears, skinned, cored, and diced**
2 Tbl	**Lemon juice**
1½ c	**Apple juice (3 apples, juiced)**
2 Tbl	**Avocado, mashed**
2 Tbl	**Banana, mashed**

1. Put the diced pears into a small bowl and stir in the lemon juice.
2. Blend the apple juice with the avocado and the banana. Pour the blended mixture over the pears and stir them together. Enjoy as is or chill slightly before serving. Garnish with a thin lemon slice or slivers.

SERVES: 2

Chilled Papaya Mint Bisque

An exotic and delicious appetizing first course.
The papaya, mint and lime create a delightful combination. Papayas are rich
in the digestive enzyme papain, vitamins A, C, and potassium.

1/4 c	**Fresh mint leaves, torn**
2½ medium	**Chilled Hawaiian papayas, seeded**
1/2 - 2/3 c	**Filtered water**
2	**Limes, juiced**
2 Tbl	**Frozen pineapple juice concentrate**

Pulse chop the mint in a food processor. Scrape the papaya flesh from its skin, put the papaya flesh into a food processor and pulse chop. Add the remaining ingredients and puree well.

SERVING SUGGESTION:
Spoon into 4 goblets and top with a tablespoon of Vanilla Cashew Creme
(page 235), a mint leaf and 1/2 a red grape for a stunning presentation.

SERVES: 4

Curried Peach Bisque

*The delicate peach flavor is enhanced by a bit of curry and ginger,
whipped in a creamy base of nut milk.*

3   **Peaches, pitted and peeled**
1 c **Almond Milk (page 57)**
1 tsp **Curry powder**
1 tsp **Ginger, skinned and minced**
2 tsp **Maple syrup (or 3 soaked dates)**

Cut the peaches into the blender. Add the remaining ingredients and puree well. Enjoy immediately or serve chilled. Garnish with a thin slice of orange.

YIELDS: 2 cups

Kiwiberry Soup

*A creamy pink soup with the tang of kiwi and a hint of vanilla.
Kiwis are high in potassium and vitamin C.*

4   **Kiwis, peeled and chopped**
1 c **Almond or Vanilla Milk (page 57)**
1 c **Frozen strawberries**
1/2 c **Sliced fresh strawberries**

Puree the kiwis, nut milk and frozen strawberries in a food processor. Pour the puree over the sliced strawberries, reserving a few for garnish on top. Add a mint leaf on top.

SERVES: 2 to 3. Makes 2 cups

Alfalfa Fennel Soup

A light, cooling soup.

1 c	Fennel juice
1/2 c	Cucumber juice (1/2 cucumber)
1 c	Alfalfa sprouts (or try onion/alfalfa)
4 Tbl	Avocado, mashed
1 tsp	Onion powder
1 tsp	Lemon juice
1/2 tsp	Garlic, minced
1 Tbl	Fresh dill, minced (or 1 tsp dried)
1 tsp	Liquid aminos
3/4 c	Cucumber, peeled, seeded, and diced

1. Put the vegetable juices, sprouts, avocado, spices, and 1/4 cup of the peeled cucumber in a blender. Blend well. (This is the soup.)
2. Put the remaining cucumber in a bowl and pour the soup on top. Stir together the soup and the cucumber, then refrigerate. Garnish with a fennel sprig. You may add cayenne or a bit of diced jalapeño as a garnish if you like it "spicy."

SERVES: 2

Almond Corn Wowder

A creamy corn chowder that is rich tasting and fulfilling. Choose sweet fresh corn off the cob and freshly made almond milk to create this wonderful soup.

2 c	Corn, cut off the cob
1½ c	Almond Milk (page 57)
1/4 c	Avocado, diced
1 Tbl	Onion, minced
1 tsp	Liquid aminos
1/2 tsp	Cumin

Put all of the ingredients into a blender and puree well. Top each serving with a garnish of: paprika, and minced fresh cilantro or dill.

If you like "spicy," add minced jalapeño chile sprinkled on top also.

YIELDS: 3½ cups—2 large servings

Beet Polarity Soup

A balancing soup of beets pureed with avocado and spices. The avocado compliments the beet, and the two blend into one delicious flavor.

1 c	**Beets, chopped**
1 c	**Filtered water (or more to taste)**
1/3 c	**Avocado, mashed**
2 tsp	**Lemon juice**
1/2 tsp	**Liquid aminos or miso**
1/2 tsp	**Dill weed**
1	**Garlic clove, pressed**

Puree everything in a blender until creamy. The small bits of beet will create some desirable textures. Serve with additional dill on top.

SERVES: 1

Borscht

A light and nutritious takeoff on the classic cold beet soup. Sprouts and fresh beet juice make this a strengthening tonic—delicious!

1/2 c	**Beets, finely grated**
1 c	**Beet juice**
1 c	**Filtered water**
1/4 c	**Green onions, chopped**
1 c	**Alfalfa sprouts**
1 tsp	**Dill weed**
1 tsp	**Onion powder**
Garnish: 1/4 c	**Green apple, peeled and diced**

1. Put the grated beets in a bowl.
2. Liquefy the remaining ingredients (except garnish) in a blender. Pour the blended liquid over the beets, stir together. Refrigerate until cold.
3. Toss the apples with a bit of lemon juice to prevent discoloration. Add a few of the apples on top of each serving.

SERVING SUGGESTION:
Try serving with Hot House Cucumber Almond Salad *(page 91) for a great meal.*

YIELDS: 3 cups. Serves 2 to 3

Creamy Escarole Soup

Escarole is one of the highest vegetarian sources for iron, 39 mg per cup. Mint, cilantro and lime balance the strong flavor of escarole, while avocado makes a creamy base. A very nutritious soup!

1/2 bunch	Escarole, sliced (or spinach)
1 c	Filtered water
1/2 medium	Avocado, chopped
1	Garlic clove, pressed
2	Green onions, chopped
2 tsp	Liquid aminos
1 Tbl	Lime juice
1½ Tbl	Dried mint, crumbled
1/3 c packed	Cilantro leaves, chopped
3/4 c	Tomato or vegetable juice
1/3 c	Nutritional yeast flakes

1. Pulse chop half of the escarole in a food processor, then add the filtered water. Add the remaining escarole and puree.
2. Add the remaining ingredients and puree well, adding water to taste.
3. Chill for a couple of hours before serving. Top with slices of mushroom or a lemon slice.

YIELDS: 4 1-cup servings

OTHER QUICK SOUP IDEAS

Just about any vegetable can be combined with avocado and blended into a tasty, healthy soup. Follow the proportions for *Beet Polarity Soup* (page 178), yet substitute carrots, zucchini, yam, or tomato for the beets. Instead of dill, you may also try basil, onion, oregano, cilantro, or any of your favorite seasonings.

Creamy Tomato Soup

A creamy red soup that is tasty and easy to make.

3 c	Tomato juice
1 Tbl	Lemon juice
1/4 c	Avocado, mashed
1/2 c	Alfalfa sprouts
1 Tbl	Onion powder

Blend in a blender until smooth.

SERVES: 2 - 3

Cucumber Bisque

A creamy, light green cold soup that entices the palate.
A nice prelude to a spicy dish.

2	Cucumbers, partially peeled, seeded, and chopped
1	Zucchini, chopped (mixed use)
1¼ c	Almond Milk (page 57)
1/4 c	Avocado, mashed
1/4 c	Leek, chopped
1 tsp	Liquid aminos
1 tsp	Coriander seeds, ground
	Fresh or dried dill garnish

1. Puree the cucumber and half of the zucchini in a food processor. Add the remaining ingredients (except the other half cup of zucchini) and then puree until smooth. Transfer to a bowl.
2. Finely chop the remaining zucchini and stir it into the soup, then refrigerate. Garnish with dill on top of each serving.

SERVES: 4 — 1 cup servings

Curried Yam Bisque

A creamy soup sweetened by a bit of apple.
This soup has the color of a large orange harvest moon.

1 c	Yam, peeled, finely grated
1/2	Green apple, peeled and finely grated
1½ c	Classic Cashew Nut Milk (page 57)
1 tsp	Curry powder
1 tsp	Fresh mint leaves, chopped

Grate the yam and apple in a food processor. Liquefy in a blender with the remaining ingredients—float a mint leaf on top of each serving as garnish.

YIELDS: 2½ cups. Serves 2

Euphoria Soup

A live, uncooked pretty pink-colored soup, loaded with live enzymes, minerals and vitamins! Delicious! Use organically grown produce if you can.

2 medium	Beets, trimmed
2 medium	Carrots, trimmed
1/2 large	Cucumber, skinned
1/2 c	Avocado, mashed
1/3 c	Cilantro leaves, loosely packed
3 c	Filtered water
2 Tbl	Natural (mild) rice vinegar
1 Tbl	"Lite" soy sauce or tamari
1	Garlic clove, crushed
1	Serrano chile, stemmed, seeded
1 tsp	Onion powder
1/2 tsp	Cumin
1 c	Corn, freshly cut off of the cob

1. Finely grate the first 3 ingredients in a food processor. Transfer into a large bowl and toss.
2. Return 3 cups of the grated veggies back into the food processor (or blender) with its work blade attached. Except for the corn, puree until smooth all of the remaining ingredients with the grated veggies.
3. Pour puree into the bowl of grated veggies, add corn. Stir and serve, or chill first.

SERVING SUGGESTION:
Garnish with cilantro leaves and lemon wedge.

SERVES: A meal for 2, or a first course for 4.

Garden Ginger Energy Soup

Live, uncooked foods contain the maximum vitamins and life force; if you tire of chewing pounds of veggies, try blending them into a delicious refreshing soup.

1½ c	Cucumber, skin, seed and chop
1 bunch	Spinach leaves, rinsed and torn in half
1 c	Filtered water
1/2 c	Avocado, mashed
1 Tbl	Ginger, peeled and minced
2½ Tbl	Lemon juice
2 tsp	"Lite" soy sauce (or Liquid aminos)
Dash	Cayenne pepper
1 c	Zucchini, finely grated
1 c	Corn kernels, cut off of cob (1 ear)

1. Put the first 3 items into a food processor and pulse chop, then blend in the avocado and spices. Puree until smooth. Scrape into a medium-size bowl.
2. Stir in the corn and zucchini and season to taste. Chill until ready to serve.

SERVES: 4

Gazpacho

A tomato garden soup, refreshing and energizing. Plan to make this the night before or in the morning so there is enough time to serve it well chilled.

2 c	Tomatoes, chopped
1/2 c	Red onion, chopped
1 c	Cucumber, peeled, seeded and chopped
1 large	Garlic clove, halved
1/2 c	Green pepper, chopped
1½ c	Tomato juice (or vegetable blend)
1/2 c each	Bell pepper (green and red or yellow), minced
1/3 c	Red onion, minced
1 c	Cucumber, peeled, seeded, diced small
1½ c	Filtered water
1 tsp	Basil or dill
1/4 c	Green onions, minced (save some for garnish)
Dash	Sea salt and cayenne or paprika

1. Put the first 5 ingredients into a food processor and puree. Transfer to a large bowl.
2. Stir in the remaining ingredients and then chill for several hours before serving.

MAKES: 4 - 5 bowls

Hearty Lentil Soup

A luscious creamy base of Almond Milk and avocado is seasoned with onion, peppers, and dill to create a hearty sprouted lentil soup.

2 Tbl	Onion, minced
1/4 c	Bell pepper, diced
1/2 c	Avocado, chopped
1 c	Almond Milk (page 57)
1/2 c	Tomato, seeded and chopped
1	Garlic clove, minced
2 Tbl	Fresh dill, minced
1 tsp	Liquid aminos
1 c	Sprouted lentils
A dash	Cayenne pepper

1. Put all of the ingredients (except the lentil sprouts) into a food processor and blend. (This is the soup.)
2. Put half of the lentil sprouts into the food processor, and pulse chop two or three quick times, just enough to mix in.
3. Pour the soup into a bowl, stir in the remaining lentil sprouts. Garnish each serving with paprika, minced fresh dill, and a few diced tomatoes.

NOTE: To make a heartier soup, you may add 1 cup corn cut from the cob and add another half cup of nut milk.

YIELDS: 3¼ cups—2 servings

Minted Carrot Soup

A slightly sweet and creamy carrot cashew soup.

1½ c	Carrots, finely grated
3 Tbl	Mint, chopped
1¾ c	Classic Cashew Nut Milk (page 57)
1/2 Tbl	White miso
1 Tbl	Red onion, minced
1 Tbl	Banana, mashed or date paste

Put all of the ingredients into a blender and liquefy. Serve with a mint leaf on top.

YIELDS: 2 cups. Serves 3

Spinacatto of the Sea

A creamy, gently spiced, mineral-rich spinach soup. For dulse lovers!

- 1 c   **Almond Milk (page 57)**
- 1/3 c   **Dulse**
- 1/2   **Avocado**
- 1 c   **Spinach leaves, torn**
- 1/3 c   **Dulse, soaked in filtered water to soften**

Blend the first four ingredients and serve the blended soup over the soaked dulse, top with cayenne (to taste). You may add hot filtered water to the soup for a warm version.

SERVES: 1

Sprouty-Strone

The dulse helps to thicken this veggie tomato soup.

- 1 c   **Filtered water**
- 2 c   **Tomatoes, chopped**
- 2 c   **Sprouts (use any sprouts on hand)**
- 1/4 c   **Dulse**
- 2   **Garlic cloves**
- 1 tsp   **Quick-Sip**
- 1/3 c   **Green onion, chopped**
- 1/3 c   **Fresh basil, chopped**
- 1/3 c   **Red pepper, chopped**
- 1/3 c   **Green pepper, minced**

1. Put the water, tomatoes, and dulse into a food processor and pulse chop to a puree.
2. Add the remaining ingredients (except the green pepper) and blend again.
3. Transfer to a bowl, stir in the bell peppers and refrigerate.

YIELDS: 2¾ cups

Zucchini Bisque

A lively, creamy green soup, spiced with lemon and dill.

1/4 c	**Red onion, chopped**
1/3 c	**Avocado, mashed**
1 tsp	**Dill weed**
1 c	**Rejuvelac Lemonade (page 169)**
1	**Garlic clove**
2 tsp	**White Miso**
1 Tbl	**Olive oil**
2½ Tbl	**Lemon juice**
1 c	**Zucchini, chopped**
	Cayenne, to taste

Blend in a blender. Refrigerate and serve cold with a dollop of *Dream de la Cream* (page 166) or *Cashew Seed Cheese Yogurt* (page 165).

YIELDS: 2¼ cups (2 servings)

Live Entrees

And now, introducing the stars of our Vibrant Living Show: the innovative, the unusual, the enchanting, the mouth-watering "entrees."

Presenting one of our favorite performances is a raw **Sweet Potato "Pasta"** topped with a super fresh **Tomato Basil Sauce;** doing a take off on the classic "angelhair pasta with tomatoes and basil." Visually resembling the Italian original, yet taking it to a new level of enjoyment.

Other standouts are the **Spicy Chile Beans** and **Black Bean Fiesta Salad** which feature sprouted beans and all the flavors of Mexico and the Southwest.

Blended to create a mousse-like consistency are sprouted lentils and avocado rolled in sliced almonds, appearing as the **Lentil Almond Log.**

Broccoli, cast as **Fleur de Broccoli,** never tasted so good! Minced broccoli with celery and onions are blended with a **Creamy Cilantro Cashew Sauce.** The mixture becomes the center of a flower on your plate, while using green snow peas as "petals."

May these mouth-watering warm-up acts prepare you for the following feature presentations! We hope these multi-ethnic flavors entertain you and inspire your own creations of live food extravaganzas!

Live Entrees

♥ FAT FREE

Black Bean Fiesta Salad

A deliciously fulfilling salad that is a celebration of Southwestern flavors.

Salad Base:	5	Romaine leaves, sliced
	1/4 head	Green cabbage, shredded coarse
	1	Carrot, sliced thin
	1/2	Zucchini, julienne
	1/2 c	Red cabbage, sliced
	1/2 c	Cucumber, quarter and slice
	1/2 bunch	Cilantro, chopped
	1 c	Creamy Soaked Seed Sauce (page 143)

Spicy Black Beans:	3/4 c	Red Chile Sauce (page 145)
	1 c	Black beans, sprouted
	1 c	Aduki or mung beans, sprouted
	1	Tomato, chopped
	1/4 c	Red onion, minced

1. Toss the salad base ingredients together and drizzle with 1/2 of the *Creamy Soaked Seed Sauce*. (Do this on one large platter or on 3 individual plates.)
2. Toss the spicy black bean mixture together and put it on top of the salad base. Drizzle the rest of the seed sauce on top.

SERVES: 3

Carrot Lentil Burgers

Serve these dehydrated burgers with
Tomato Basil Sauce (page 145) and a leafy salad.

2 c	Carrots, grated
1 c	Sprouted lentils
1 c	Sprouted wheat berries
1 Tbl	White miso
1 Tbl	Onion powder
1	Garlic clove, pressed
1 tsp	Coriander powder
1 tsp	Cumin seeds
2/3 c	Filtered water

Pulse chop the lentil and wheat berry sprouts together in a food processor. Add the rest of the ingredients and blend them well. Form into patties 1/2″ thick by 4″ on a plastic-lined food dehydrator tray. Dehydrate for 12 hours on the bottom tray or until dry on top.

YIELDS: 6 to 7 patties

Cauliflower Seed Cheese Loaf

This light vegetable loaf is loaded with enzymes found within the seed cheese. It is very easy to prepare and mound into any desired shape. A delicious buffet entree when served with your favorite sauce on the side.

1 medium	Cauliflower, chopped
2 ribs	Celery, chopped
1/2 c	Red onion, chopped
1 c	Seasoned Nut Cheese* (page 167)
1 tsp	Dill weed
1 tsp	Caraway seeds
1/2 Tbl	Lemon juice
1/2 tsp	Paprika
1 tsp	Dry mustard

1. Put the cauliflower, celery, and onion into a food processor and pulse chop them until they are finely ground. You may have to do this in 2 batches depending on the size of your food processor's work bowl.
2. Add the remaining ingredients to the food processor and blend them in well. Transfer the mixture into a mold, or a bowl, if you are molding by hand.
3. Unmold the loaf, or mound mixture onto a bed of greens, such as shredded kale, or lettuce leaves. Drizzle a sauce on top of the vegetable loaf, then lay tomato slices on top. Top with fresh dill sprigs. Serve extra sauce on the side.

*You may add more garlic, dill, or lemon to taste.

SERVES: 4

RECOMMENDED SAUCES:
Try Spicy Cucumber Garden Dressing *(page 116),* Lemon Tahini Sauce *(page 144), or* Cilantro Cashew Sauce *(page 142).*

Cracked Wheat Jubilee

A grain salad spiced with ginger and tossed with mushrooms, bell pepper, apple, and papaya. Makes a lovely light dinner or lunch.

2/3 c	**Cracked wheat (bulgur)**
2/3 c	**Hot filtered water**
3	**Mushrooms, sliced**
1 small	**Green Apple, diced small**
1 Tbl	**Ginger, skinned and minced or grated**
1 tsp	**Dr. Bronner's Bouillon or tamari**
1/2	**Lime, juiced**
1/8 tsp	**Cayenne**
1/4	**Papaya, skinned and chopped**
1/2	**Bell pepper, diced**
3 Tbl	**Salad dressing of your choice***

Optional garnish:

3 Tbl	**Cashew pieces**

1. Cover the wheat with the hot filtered water. Let it sit covered in a small bowl until soft, about 15 minutes.
2. Add the remaining ingredients and then toss well. Serve with extra papaya spears, an extra side of salad dressing, and sprouts. Top with cashews.

*Try *Curried Pumpkin Dressing,* page 108 or *Light Cucumber Dressing,* page 111.

SERVES: 2

Curried Tomato Cups

A wonderfully subtle curry-flavored filling of lentil sprouts,
cashews, sunflower seeds, ginger, currants, and cumin seeds really
make this a winner! Use also as a sandwich filling.

2 very large	**Tomatoes, 1/2˝ of top cut off***

Curried filling:

1/4 c	**Sunflower seeds, raw**
1/4 c	**Cashews, raw**
1 tsp	**Ginger, skinned and freshly grated**
1	**Garlic clove, pressed**
2/3 c	**Lentil sprouts**
1/4 c	**Red onion, chopped**
2 tsp	**Curry powder**
2 tsp	**Cumin seeds**
2 Tbl	**Currants**
Garnish:	**Coconut shreds, currants, cilantro sprig**

*Save tomato tops for another salad.

1. Cut around the inside perimeter of each tomato halve with a knife, loosening the pulp. Slice an "X" shape into each half, careful not to cut into bottom of tomato. Invert each tomato half over the sink and squeeze out seeds. Spoon the tomato flesh into a food processor (2/3 cup tomato pulp).
2. Finely grind the sunseeds and cashews in a nut grinder until they are powdery smooth. Put the powder into a food processor.
3. Add the remaining ingredients, except for the currants, and quickly pulse chop them all together until a thick paste forms. Pulse chop in the currants (do not overmix). Fill the tomato cups with the curried filling and garnish.

SERVING SUGGESTIONS:
Put each tomato cup onto a plate, surround it with alfalfa sprouts, sunflower greens, carrot sticks, and a lemon wedge. Serve your favorite salad dressing on the side.

SERVES: 2

English Garden Tomato Ring

A "gelled" salad spiked with petite green peas and cucumber. A warm weather delight because it is light and cooling to the palate.

3 c	Tomato juice
1½ Tbl	Avocado, mashed
2 Tbl	Lemon juice
1/2 c	Alfalfa sprouts
1 Tbl	Onion powder
1/2 c	Agar flakes
1 c	Filtered water
1 c	English cucumber, diced small
1 c	Petite green peas (defrost if using frozen)

1. Blend the first five ingredients in a blender until smooth. Pour the mixture into a medium bowl.
2. Dissolve the agar flakes in the filtered water in a small saucepan and bring the mixture to a boil. Boil for 1 minute undisturbed, then quickly whisk into the tomato mixture.
3. Pour the agar-tomato mixture into a ring mold, sprinkle in the cucumber and the peas. Refrigerate until firm, then unmold on a plate. Garnish with a ring of alfalfa sprouts around the tomato gel and top with avocado slices.

SERVES: 4

Fleur de Broccoli

*This entree consists of a minced broccoli salad dressed with
a creamy* Cilantro Cashew Sauce *(page 142). Serve garnished with
a sweet salad of hiziki and snow peas. This salad is arranged to resemble a flower,
the snow peas are placed around the broccoli salad as petals.*

3 c	Broccoli, finely minced
1 c	Celery, sliced
1/2 c	Red onions, minced
1/2 c	Broccoli "florettes" (small crowns)
1 recipe	Cilantro Cashew Sauce (page 142)
1 recipe	Sweet-Ziki (page 98)
1 c	Snow peas, trimmed
Garnish	Tomato wedges

1. Pulse chop the broccoli in a food processor, measure, and put it into a large bowl. Halve the celery stalks lengthwise, then slice and add to the bowl. Toss in the red onions and the broccoli florettes.

2. Arrange some leafy greens on individual plates. Press the broccoli salad into a measuring cup and invert it onto the plates. Arrange the hiziki salad in a half circle around the salad, then place the snow peas radiating out on the other half, like the petals of a flower.

SERVES: 2 to 3

Green Bean Tomato Salad

*Sprouted aduki beans tossed with tomatoes and green beans
in a fresh and lively marinade. The combination of sprouted red aduki beans along
with green beans makes for a hearty meal.*

2 c	**Green beans, trimmed**
1 c	**Tomato, chopped and seeded**
2 Tbl	**Red onion, slice thin and chop**
1 c	**Aduki bean sprouts**
2 Tbl	**Lemon juice**
1 Tbl	**Virgin olive oil**
1/4 tsp	**Cracked black pepper**
1/4 tsp	**Rosemary, crushed**
1/2 tsp	**Mustard, dry**
1 tsp	**Tamari or liquid aminos**
Optional: 1/2 c	**Mushrooms, sliced**

Slice the green beans lengthwise and then chop by slicing them on an angle into
1˝ pieces. Toss all of the ingredients together in a medium sized bowl.

SERVING SUGGESTION:
*Serve on butter lettuce leaves, along with dehydrated crackers,
and a seasoned nut cheese (page 167).*

SERVES: 2

Imperial Salad

Crisp bean sprouts create the backbone of this refreshing Oriental salad loaded with vegetables and hiziki seaweed.

1/3 c	**Hiziki (dried seaweed)**
2/3 c	**Warm filtered water**
3 c	**Mushrooms, sliced**
1/2 c	**Celery, diced or sliced on angle**
2	**Green onions, sliced on angle**
4 c	**Bean sprouts, wash and spin dry**
1 c	**Carrots, shredded**
1 c	**Cabbage, grated finely**
1 recipe	**Gingered Cashew Sauce (page 149)**
Garnish: 1/2 c	**Cashew pieces**
1/4 c	**Cilantro leaves**

1. Soak the hiziki in warm filtered water for 10 to 15 minutes (until soft). Rinse and drain a couple of times. Put the hiziki into a large bowl.
2. Prepare the vegetables and put them into the large bowl. Toss the *Gingered Cashew Sauce* into the vegetables and hiziki until they are well coated.
3. Refrigerate and garnish with cashews and cilantro.

SERVING SUGGESTIONS
For a dinner, add Spicy Sprout Salad *(page 96),* Sweet-Ziki *(page 98), or a soup along with* Garden Crisps *(page 126).*

SERVES: 4

Italian Deli Salad

This is a colorful chopped salad served with a tasty vinaigrette using varied produce cut in large pieces. Feel free to substitute ingredients with what is super fresh and colorful to create a visual rainbow.

4 c	Spinach leaves, torn
6	Radicchio leaves
1	Beet, finely shredded
3 baby	Zucchini, sliced
1 large	Tomato, wedged
1	Carrot, sliced
1/2	Red pepper, chopped coarse
1/2 c	Sprouts

1. Divide the spinach onto 2 plates. Place 3 radicchio leaves as "cups" around each spinach salad. Divide the next 3 vegetables in half by placing half of the beets in one "cup," the zucchini in another "cup," and the sprouts in the third "cup."
2. Sprinkle carrot slices and the bell pepper over the spinach leaves. Wedge tomatoes in between radicchio "cups." Drizzle *Olive Garlic Vinaigrette* (page 112) on top.

SERVING SUGGESTIONS
Top with Pecan Basil Pesto *(page 150) and some* Sprouted Herb Crackers *(page 129) for a wonderful meal.*

SERVES: 2

Japanese Buddhist Delight

This is a fun meal, because it consists of many bowls of uniquely marinated or seasoned vegetables. Guests get to pick and choose from the pickled, the sweet, the savory and the spicy. Use fresh vegetables to create a lazy susan-style meal. For more elaborate meals, include some vegetable sushi rolls from the chapter "Snackin' on the Wild Side." Other delicious side dishes are: Sweet-Ziki (page 98).

Daikon Salad

A crisp, crunchy, and refreshing salad.

1	Daikon, 6˝ long, peeled
1/2	Avocado, sliced
2 Tbl	Cilantro leaves, minced

Sauce:

2 Tbl	Lime juice
1 tsp	Tamari
1 tsp	Sesame oil

1. Finely shred the daikon into a long pasta-like shape. Use a "Kitchen Help" device or cut by hand. Put the daikon "pasta" into a bowl and top with avocado and cilantro.
2. Stir together the sauce and pour it on top of the salad.

Wakame Sesame Salad

A serving of various sea vegetables is a must! Wakame contains a high quantity of vitamin B_{12}.

2½ c	Wakame, soaked and rinsed
1 Tbl	Lime juice
1 Tbl	Brown sesame seeds (unhulled)
Dash	Sea seasoning (dulse or kelp)

1. Stir all of the ingredients together in a medium bowl.
2. Garnish with red pepper strips and more sesame seeds.

Ginger Oyster Mushroom

Savory marinated mushrooms.

1 c	Oyster mushrooms, torn into large pieces
1½ tsp	Ginger, skinned and grated
1/2 Tbl	Lime juice
1/2 Tbl	Tamari
1 tsp	Maple syrup

1. Put the oyster mushrooms into a bowl.
2. Stir together the remaining marinade ingredients and pour the stirred mixture over the mushrooms.
3. Toss all of the ingredients together and let it marinate for a couple of hours, or overnight in the fridge.

King Neptune's Sea Loaf

A sprouted lentil and sea vegetable loaf served with a Lemon Tahini Sauce *(page 144). This can be served as a loaf or as individual croquettes.*

8 oz	**Sea palm fronds (yields 2 cups soaked sea vegetables)**
3 sticks	**Wakame**
2 ribs	**Celery, trimmed and chopped**
1/3 c	**Soaked almonds**
2 tsp	**Garlic, chopped**
1 c	**Lentil sprouts**
1½ Tbl	**Minced dried onion**
1 heaping tsp	**Freshly grated ginger root (skinned first)**
3 tsp	**Tamari**
1 c	**Finely grated carrot**
1 Tbl each	**Cilantro and green onions, minced**
1/4 c	**Bell pepper, minced**

1. Cover the sea vegetables with filtered water and soak for 30 minutes.
2. Pulse chop the celery with the almonds and garlic in a food processor, add the sea vegetables, tamari, ginger and lentils and blend for a minute until a paste-like consistency forms. Transfer to a bowl.
3. Attach a fine grater to the food processor and grate the carrot. Stir into the sea vegetable mixture along with the cilantro, chives and green bell pepper.

SERVING SUGGESTION:

Press into a 1/2 cup form, invert on a lettuce leaf, remove the cup, then top the individual croquettes with Lemon Tahini Sauce *(page 144) and a cilantro sprig.*

Sea Loaf "Boats"

Serve the Sea Loaf in 1/2 of a red or green bell pepper, then top with *Lemon Tahini Sauce* (page 144).

Lentil Almond Log

This mousse-like loaf makes a beautiful live foods presentation, because it is rolled in sliced almonds. Serve it surrounded with alfalfa sprouts, sliced tomatoes, and cucumbers, and a sauce such as Tomato Basil Sauce *(page 145) or* Lemon Tahini Sauce *(page 144). A royal feast!*

Lentil Log:	2½ c	**Lentil Sprouts**
	1/2 c	**Parsley, chopped**
	1/2 c	**Celery, chopped**
	1/4 c	**Onion, chopped**
	1½ Tbl	**Mellow miso**
	1/2 c	**Avocado, mashed**
	1 tsp	**Garlic, minced**
	1/4 c	**Oat bran**
	1/2 Tbl	**Lemon juice**
	1/2 tsp	**Nori sea seasoning**
Agar binder:	2 Tbl	**Agar flakes**
	1/3 c	**Filtered water**
Garnish:	1/2 c	**Sliced almonds**

1. Put all of the lentil log ingredients into a food processor and pulse chop to blend. Stop and scape down the sides of the food processor, then continue blending until thoroughly mixed.
2. Stir the agar into the filtered water in a small saucepan. Bring mixture to a boil for 1 minute, then remove from the heat. Turn the food processor on, and while the machine is running, slowly pour agar liquid into the lentil mixture.
3. Spoon the lentil mixture onto a lightly oiled sheet of wax paper or foil, and roll up the lentil mixture into a log. Tuck in the ends of the wrapped log and place it in a bread pan. Refrigerate for a minimum of 1 hour.
4. Unwrap the log and spread out the sliced almonds in front, and proceed to roll lentil log in almonds until it is completely covered with almonds. Place on a platter, decorate it, and slice to serve.

SERVES: 4 to 6

Millet Burgers

A savory dehydrated grain burger to crumble over a salad or serve as a separate entree. The celery and sprouted millet give this burger a crunch.

3 c	Sprouted millet*
1 c	Celery, minced
1 c	Sprouted wheat
1/3 c	Tahini
1/4 c	Red onion, chopped
2	Garlic cloves, pressed
1 Tbl	Tamari
1/3 c	Filtered water
2 tsp each	Cumin and oregano

1. Pulse chop all of the ingredients except the celery and the millet in a food processor, then blend them well.
2. Quickly pulse chop in the millet, stir in the celery.
3. Form the mixture into grain burgers on lined food dehydrator trays. Dry for 24 hours.

To serve: top each grain burger with a thick slice of tomato and serve with *Peanut Sauce* (page 144), *Creamy Pesto Sauce* (page 143), or *Cheezy Cashew Sauce* (page 142). Serve with a salad of your choice, or with *Arugula Spinach Salad* (page 87)..

*1 cup millet = 3 cups sprouted millet

Pandora's Salad

A curious salad of seasoned seaweed and shredded vegetables,
topping a bed of greens. The more you eat, the more you want . . .

1 oz	Wakame, dried seaweed
1 large	Carrot
1	Zucchini
10	Button mushrooms, sliced

Sauce: 1½	Limes, juiced
½ tsp	Chile sesame oil
2	Garlic cloves, pressed
1 Tbl	Extra virgin olive oil
1 tsp	Tamari
2 Tbl	Sesame seeds
1 Tbl	Almonds, minced
1½ Tbl	Brown rice vinegar

Bed of leafy greens:

3 c	Spinach leaves, torn
1 c	Alfalfa sprouts, separate
1 c	Arugula leaves
1	Tomato, thinly sliced

1. Cover the wakame with filtered water and let it soak in a medium bowl for 20 minutes until soft. Strain out the water, then rinse and drain again using fresh water.

2. Finely shred the carrot and zucchini in a food processor. Put the veggies and mushrooms in the bowl with the wakame. Stir together the sauce ingredients and toss the sauce into the vegetables.

3. Put the leafy greens on a platter, put the sliced tomato over the greens and mound the sea vegetable salad on top of everything. Garnish with Nori flakes or gomasio.

SERVES: 2 - 3

Ruby Beet Loaf

A ruby red and fortifying blend of dulse and beets.
This soft spread gets put on top of a large mandala salad for special
presentations—or use it to stuff celery, peppers, or tomatoes.

1/2 c	Almonds, finely ground in a food mill
1/2 c	Sesame seeds, soaked in filtered water
1 c	Rejuvelac Lemonade (page 169)
1 c	Dulse
2 medium	Beets, finely grated
1	Carrot, finely grated
1 tsp	Grated lemon peel
1 large	Garlic clove, pressed

1. Pulse chop the first four ingredients in a food processor, then blend them. Put the blended mixture into a bowl.

2. Stir in the remaining ingredients and then serve the *Ruby Beet Loaf* over a large platter of greens, such as:

1 c	Shredded beet greens
1/4 bunch	Escarole, sliced
1 c	Sprouts, pulled apart
1	Bell pepper, chopped

3. Top with your favorite sauce, or try *Creamy Pesto Sauce* (page 143), or *Lemon Tahini Sauce* (page 144).

SERVES: 3 - 4

Sea "Pasta" Vegetable Salad

A wonderful salad of various sea and land vegetables. Seaweeds are super nutritious and supply you with lots of vitamin B$_{12}$ and minerals.

1/2 oz	Sea palm or wakame (alaria), dried
1 oz	Arame, dried
4	Shiitake mushrooms, dried
2 c	Cucumber, peeled, seeded and sliced
1	Bell pepper, sliced (yellow/green)
1 large	Tomato, seeded and chopped
2 Tbl	Rice vinegar
1	Garlic clove, pressed
2 tsp	Tamari or "lite" soy sauce (or to taste)
1 Tbl	Toasted golden sesame oil

1. Put the sea vegetables and mushrooms into a large bowl. Cover with filtered water and let soak 15 minutes.
2. Stem and slice the mushrooms, set aside. Strain the sea vegetables, rinse in cool filtered water, and strain again.
3. Add the vegetables, mushrooms and the rest of the ingredients to a large bowl. Toss well and refrigerate.

SERVING SUGGESTION:
Serve on lettuce leaves with avocado slices on top.

SERVES: 2

Spicy Chile Beans

Sprout your beans ahead of time to make this sensational "live" chile.

1 c	**Red onion, chopped thin**
2 tsp	**Garlic, pressed**
1 Tbl	**Red chile powder**
1/2 Tbl	**Cumin powder**
5 Tbl	**Lemon or lime juice**
1½ Tbl	**Liquid aminos**
1/2 c	**Mung bean sprouts**
1/2 c	**Lentil sprouts**
1/2 c	**Garbanzo sprouts**
1/2 c	**Green pea sprouts**
1 c	**Tomato, minced**
Optional: 1 c	**Corn, cut form the cob**
1/2 Tbl	**Serrano chile, seeded, minced**
As garnish: 1/2 c	**Cilantro leaves, minced**

} 2 c Mixed bean sprouts

1. Mix together the ingredients from the onion to the liquid aminos in a medium bowl.
2. Add the beans and tomatoes (and the remaining items), stir well. Refrigerate for 24 hours if possible.
3. Serve over a bed of greens (baby spinach, shredded kale, etc.) with sliced avocado on top.

NOTE: Mung and lentil beans can be sprouted together. Black beans, garbanzo beans and green peas can be sprouted together.

SERVING SUGGESTIONS:
For more elaborate meals, begin with Yucatan Fruit Salad *(page 84),* and serve *Pineapple Salsa* (page 151) *on the side.*

Sprouted Lentil Loaf

A delicious salad loaf of sprouted lentils and grated veggies,
seasoned with a creamy cashew sauce.

Salad:	1	Celery stock (use inner soft ribs and leaves only)
	1/3 - 1/2 c	Red onion (approx. 1/2 onion)
	1½ c	Lentil sprouts
	1 c	Carrots, grated (approx. 2 medium)
	1/3 c	Zucchini (approx. 1/2)
Sauce:	1/3 c	Cashews, finely ground
	2½ Tbl	Filtered water
	3 Tbl	Lemon juice
	2 tsp	Tamari
	1	Garlic clove, chopped
	2 tsp	Dill weed and coriander (if fresh, use 1 Tbl each)
		Dash of cumin, curry and cayenne

1. Pulse chop the celery and onion finely in a food processor. Add the lentil sprouts and pulse chop one to three quick times (do not mash).
2. Change to a fine grate blade and grate carrots and zucchinis into the same work bowl. Transfer to a salad bowl.
3. Blend all of the sauce ingredients together and toss into the salad—form into a loaf and garnish or keep as a tossed salad. Chill.

SERVES: 4

Sweet Potato Hiziki "Pasta" Salad

This dish resembles a Pacific Rim pasta dish, however, raw sweet potatoes are used to resemble spaghettini. The "Cook Help" handcrank slicing gadget (by Beriner) creates long pasta shapes of various root vegetables, and is used here for a distinct effect.

1	Sweet potato, peeled and finely grated
1 c	Hiziki, soaked in filtered water
1 Tbl	Lime juice
1 tsp	Tamari
1/2 c	Mushrooms, thinly sliced
1/4 c	Bell peppers, minced
1/2 c	Roma tomatoes, seeded and chopped
3 Tbl	Ginger Sesame Lime Sauce (page 110)
Optional: 1/2	Serrano chile, minced
Garnish: 2 Tbl	Chives, minced

1. Use a "Kitchen Help" device to cut long thin pasta shapes from sweet potato. Divide onto two plates.
2. Put rinsed and drained hiziki into a bowl. Toss in the lime and tamari, then mix in mushrooms, peppers and tomatoes. Place 1/2 of the mixture on top of each plate of sweet potato pasta.
3. Pour *Ginger Sesame Lime Sauce* evenly on top of each serving, top with chives.

SERVES: 2

Sweet Potato "Pasta" with Tomato Basil Sauce

A wonderful fresh tomato sauce tops "pasta" that is made from finely shredded sweet potatoes. Light, sweet, and delicious! Make the tomato sauce just before serving to have a warm sauce. (The tomatoes become warm from the hot water they soak in, this loosens their skin.)

1	**Sweet potato, peeled**
1 recipe	**Tomato Basil Sauce (page 145)**

1. Finely shred the sweet potato using a "Kitchen Help" device (which cuts long, thin pasta shapes), or you may use a food processor for shorter shreds. You may also try shredding yams, squashes or jicama to create interesting colors, textures, and tastes.
2. Divide the "pasta" and place it on 2 plates. Top with the *Tomato Basil Sauce.*
3. Garnish with fresh basil or parsley; or for a richer treat, top with 1 Tbl. minced pecans or pine nuts.

Note: Use 1/2 sweet potato per serving. Cutting the sweet potato into a long, thin "pasta" shape is essential to creating the visual recognition of pasta.

SERVES: 2

Tabouli Spinach Salad

Tabouli is a Middle Eastern cracked wheat salad seasoned with parsley, mint, and lemon. Here we have added carrots, onions, and tomatoes to create a main meal.

2/3 c	Cracked wheat (or tabouli mix)*
2/3 c	Hot filtered water
1 Tbl	Mint, minced or crumbled
1 c	Carrot, coarsely shredded
1/4 c	Red onion, minced
1 c	Tomato, chopped (2 small ones)
1/4 c	Green onion, minced
1 recipe	Tomato Basil Dressing (page 118)
Optional: 1 c	Lentil or mung sprouts
	Cracked black pepper to taste
	Spinach leaves, torn

1. Cover the cracked wheat or the tabouli mix with hot filtered water in a large bowl. Let sit for 15 minutes, or until soft.
2. Toss in the vegetables and 1/2 cup of *Tomato Basil Dressing* and serve on a bed of spinach leaves. Serve with additional dressing drizzled on top, or on the side.

*If using cracked wheat, you may wish to add more seasoning, such as: a bit of parsley, onion, and garlic.

Yam Patties

These have a savory sweetness and are just as delicious raw as dehydrated. Serve with a Creamy Pesto Sauce (page 143) or a Lemon Tahini Sauce (page 144) and a salad.

3 c	**Yams or sweet potatoes, finely grated**
1/2 c	**Red onion, chopped**
1 Tbl	**White miso**
2 Tbl	**Raw tahini**
1½ tsp	**Basil**
1/2 c	**Sprouted wheat berries**
1/2 Tbl	**Barley malt or rice syrup**
4 Tbl	**Nutritional yeast flakes**

1. Finely grate the yams or sweet potatoes in a food processor. Measure and put aside the grated mixture in a bowl.
2. Put the next three items in a food processor; use a chop blade to puree. Add the sweet potatoes and the remaining ingredients to the food processor and grind them well.
3. Form the mixture into small patties and place in a food dehydrator on cheese cloth, or on a tight weave tray. Dehydrate for about eight hours or until the desired dryness is achieved. Check periodically. Lower shelves will "cook" the patties faster.

NOTE: If you press the patties out thin, they will come out more like a "cracker." Patties 1/2″ thick or so will be more of a "burger."

YIELDS: approximately 10 thick patties or 14 thin ones

Vibrant Desserts

Let the angel of sweetness awaken the wizard of desserts in your kitchen!
Delight in the magical simplicity of papaya spears, chilled grapes, or a wedge of
watermelon for dessert, or prepare a sparkling finish to a vibrant meal.

***Banana Splits with Carob Sauce** and **Chunky Monkey Sundae** are*
sweet, gooey, and spectacular fountain treats.

Mystify your palate with low-calorie cool and creamy fruity ecstasies from
***Pink Pineapple Whip** to **Cherimoya Freeze**, frozen sorbets extraordinaire!*

Visually excite your guests with gelled fruit pies and tarts as you bring them to life with
*toppings of a sublime **Vanilla Cashew Cream** or a fresh **Raspberry Sauce**.*

You will discover 10 high-energy cookies and bars that are
miraculously created from sprouted grains, seeds, fruits and nuts. "Baked" in
*a food dehydrator, they have an extended life. **Carrot Cake Raisin Bars, Sweet Energy***
***Gems**, or **Almond Macadamia Fig Bars** are perfect traveling companions and*
may be called on in a moment's notice for an instant energy lift.

May life's sweet vibrations keep you smiling.

Vibrant Desserts

Fresh Fruit Desserts

*Begin enjoying fresh, colorful, juicy fruits for dessert.
They will quench your sweet tooth and leave you with a light
(rather than a stuffed) feeling after a wonderful meal. Crisp apple wedges,
orange slices, a date, or a fig will treat your sweet tooth without added fat.
(See the* Fruit Salads *chapter for other ideas.)*

Mandala Fruit Platter

*Soak dried organic fruit (in filtered water) in separate bowls overnight
(or until rehydrated). Keep in the refrigerator until ready to use.
Soaking dried fruit makes them easier to digest.*

*Dried fruits supply lots of vitamins and minerals and
satisfy a sweet craving, while being a lowcal, nonfat treat. Mix them
with fresh orange and apple slices for texture and taste variation. Oranges
(vitamin C) help the body to efficiently utilize iron, a prevalent nutrient in
dried fruits. So remember to eat an orange with iron-rich foods.*

Soak the following fruits in filtered water:

12	**Pitted prunes**
1/3 c	**Raisins**
4 - 7	**Apricots, halved**
6 - 7	**Figs, sliced in half**

Fresh Fruit:

1	**Orange, cut in wedges**
1	**Apple, cut in wedges**
12	**Dates with an almond inside each**

Put the apple wedges in a line down the center of a platter. Put the oranges in a line crossing the apples (to form an "X" shape). Place the prunes in one quadrant, the figs in another, and the apricots and dates in the last 2 sections. Sprinkle raisins on top or put them in the center of your masterpiece!

SERVES: 4 - 6, or more

Aphrodite's Freeze

The Greek Goddess of Love and Beauty definitely would be seduced by this dessert.

1 c	Frozen apricots
1	Frozen banana
1/2 c	Orange juice

Pulse chop all of the ingredients in a food processor, then blend well until smooth. Serve immediately in small dessert cups or goblets.

SERVES: 2

Banana Almandine Cream

Smooth, creamy, and rich—definitely outrageous!

1½	Frozen bananas, chopped
1½ Tbl	Almond butter
1/2 tsp	Almond extract
1 tsp	Vanilla extract
2-3 Tbl	Almond Milk (page 57)

Put the first four ingredients into a food processor and pulse chop. Add the *Almond Milk* to desired consistency. Then puree until smooth.

SERVES: 2

Banana Ice Cream

The first all-fruit ice cream we ever made; one bite and we were in paradise!

| 2 | Bananas, frozen, chopped |

1. Blend or puree in a food processor.
2. Stop and stir till thick and creamy, serve immediately.

SERVES: 1

Banana Split with Carob Sauce

Creamy banana "ice cream" is scooped over a split banana, top it off with carob sauce and some chopped nuts for a real treat!

2 large	Bananas, chopped and frozen
2 Tbl	Almond Milk (page 57)
1	Banana, split in half lengthwise
1-2 Tbl	Carob Sauce (page 234)
1 Tbl	Walnuts or almonds, chopped

1. Blend the frozen bananas with *Almond Milk* in a food processor until creamy.
2. Put the split banana into a dish and top it with the frozen banana "ice cream."
3. Top with the *Carob Sauce* and chopped nuts . . . eat immediately!

YIELDS: 1 split

Cherimoya Freeze

A true delicacy! Cherimoyas have a custard apple flavor with hints of lemon.

2 medium	Cherimoyas, peeled

1. Put the peeled Cherimoyas into a strainer. (Use one with a medium-coarse screen.) Using the back of a spoon, press the fruit through the strainer holes. Do this over a bowl to catch the "spooned" puree.
2. Alternately press and stir until all that is left are the Cherimoya seeds. Discard them.
3. Divide the puree into 2 dessert cups and put in the freezer for 2 hours before serving.

SERVES: 2

Chunky Monkey Sundae

If you go ape over peanut butter and bananas, you'll love this!

1½	**Frozen bananas, chopped**
1½ Tbl	**Peanut butter**
1/2 Tbl	**Raw carob powder**
1/4 c	**Almond Milk (page 57)**
1 Tbl	**Maple syrup (optional)**
1/2 recipe	**Carob Sauce (page 234)**
Garnish: 1 Tbl	**Pecans or peanuts, chopped**

Pulse chop all of the ingredients (except *Carob Sauce*) in a food processor, puree till smooth. Spoon into 2 dessert glasses and top with the *Carob Sauce* and a few chopped peanuts or pecans.

SERVES: 2

Just Peachy

A delightful frozen dessert—light, fragrant and delicious.
Substitute the papaya with mango for another nice treat.

2 c	**Frozen peaches, or nectarines**
1/2	**Ripe banana**
1/3 c	**Papaya pulp**
Topping: 3 Tbl	**Papaya, chopped**
1	**Lime wedge per person**

1. Partially defrost the frozen fruit quickly by soaking the bag in boiling water for a couple of minutes.
2. Put the peaches into a food processor and pulse chop them until they are broken into small pieces. Add the remaining ingredients and continue to puree until smooth.
3. Spoon into desert cups and top with fresh papaya and a squeeze of lime on top.

SERVES: 3 or 4

Mango Cream

*A heavenly frozen ice cream made with just mangos and almond milk.
It whips up in seconds in your food processor. Mangos are an excellent source
of vitamin A and supply lots of vitamin C, beta-carotene, iron,
magnesium, and potassium. They are ripe May–September.*

8 oz	**Frozen mango chunks**
5 Tbl	**Almond Milk (page 57)**

Pulse chop mangos in your food processor with 2 Tbl of *Almond Milk*. When softened, add the remaining *Almond Milk* and puree until creamy.

SERVES: 2

Piña Colada Sorbet

A tropical low-cal sorbet.

2 c	**Pineapple chunks**
1	**Banana**
1/4 c	**Pineapple-coconut juice or orange juice**

1. Freeze the pineapple chunks overnight.
2. Blend or puree the pineapple chunks with the banana, adding the juice slowly. Stop and stir until all is pureed—put the puree into glasses or dessert cups and freeze for 1 hour before serving.

SERVES: 4

Pink Pineapple Whip

A sweet, refreshing and pink-colored pineapple frozen dessert.

3	**Whole strawberries, frozen**
1 c	**Pineapple chunks, frozen**
1	**Banana, frozen, chopped**
3/4 c	**Pineapple juice**

Pulse chop all of the ingredients in a food processor using 1/4 cup of pineapple juice, puree. Add the remaining pineapple juice and puree until smooth

SERVES: 2

Purple Mint Passion

A cooling treat.

1/3 c	**Cashews, soaked**
1½ c	**Frozen blueberries**
2 Tbl	**Maple syrup**
	Few drops peppermint oil or extract

Blend all of the ingredients until smooth—great after fiery spicy foods. Thin to desired consistency by adding 1 to 3 Tbl of nut milk.

SERVES: 2

Strawberry Nut Ice Cream

Soaking the cashews for 8 to 10 hours causes the cashews to release their oils, which float to the surface of the water. Soaking decreases the oil content of cashews and makes them easier to blend to a creamy smooth puree in a blender. This mixture very much resembles ice cream.

1 c	**Raw cashew pieces**
	Filtered water to cover
1/3 c	**Dates, pitted, with filtered water to cover (7)**
11	**Frozen strawberries**
1/2 tsp	**Vanilla**
1	**Frozen banana**

1. Soak the cashews overnight in filtered water. Soak the dates in filtered water overnight (use a separate bowl). Rinse and strain cashews before putting them into a blender.
2. Blend the cashews and the dates with their soak water in the blender until creamy. Add the remaining ingredients and blend well.
3. Pour into dessert cups and freeze one hour. Top with sliced fresh strawberries.

SERVES: 4

Strawberry Orange Sorbet

Fresh, fruity, and delicious.

12	**Frozen strawberries**
4	**Dates, pitted**
1/2 c	**Orange juice**

Puree all of the ingredients together, top with raisins and some oat flakes, if desired.

SERVES: 2

Almond Pie Crust

A heavenly pie crust, versatile for any fresh fruit filling. The ground oat flakes absorb any excess moisture from the soaked almonds, creating a perfect consistency. Use leftover pie dough for a cookie base, just add dried fruit. For a smaller pie, use half of the ingredients called for.

2 c	**Soaked almonds, drained well**
1 c	**Date nuggets or pieces**
1 c	**Ground cashews or sunflower seeds**
1/2 c	**Oat flakes, ground into a powder**

1. Grind almonds and dates in a food processor until a paste is formed. Add the remaining ingredients to the food processor and blend them well. Lightly oil a pie dish.
2. Roll out the dough between 2 layers of plastic wrap or wax paper (1/8" to 1/4" thick), so that it extends 1" beyond the outer edge of the pie dish.
3. Peel off the top layer of the plastic wrap and center the inverted pie dish over the dough. Hold on to both the dough and the pie dish and flip them right side up together.
4. Peel off the outer layer of plastic wrap and gently press the dough into the pie dish.

YIELD: 9½˝ deep dish pie crust, or 2 smaller crusts

Fresh Fruit Ring

A beautiful low-cal fresh fruit mold.

2 baskets	Sweet fresh strawberries, sliced
2	Peaches, sliced
6 oz	Fresh fruit smoothie (or 1¾ c juice blended with 2 very ripe or frozen bananas)
1/8 c	Coconut, shredded
1½ Tbl	Agar flakes
1/2 c	Filtered water

1. Mix the filtered water and agar flakes. Bring to a boil with some of the juice—stir and simmer.
2. Put the sliced fruit in a bowl—pour in the remaining juice and agar—mix thoroughly.
3. Pour into a decorative ring and chill in the freezer for 1 ½ hours, then serve—or refrigerate several hours before serving.

SERVING SUGGESTION:
Invert on a pretty crystal or glass plate, decorate with flowers or sliced fruit.

SERVES: 4

Fresh Fruit Tart

A spiraling assortment of colorful fruit glistening under a fresh glaze. You can serve this on a raw crust or by itself as a jelled dessert—either way it's delicious.

6	Peaches or nectarines, peeled and sliced
8	Whole strawberries, tops trimmed
2	Kiwis, peeled and sliced
1 basket	Raspberries
2 c	Fruit juice
2 Tbl	Agar flakes
Optional	Almond Pie Crust (page 223)

1. Prepare the fruit, wash and pat dry. Arrange the fruit in a 9˝ to 10˝ glass pie or quiche dish (or, do this over a pie crust if desired): Peaches on the perimeter, strawberries in the next row, kiwis in the third row and raspberries in the center of the circle (or any other way that alternates the colors with whatever fresh fruit is on hand).
2. Dissolve the agar flakes in the fruit juice, then bring to a boil for 1 minute. Reduce and simmer for a few minutes, then set aside for a couple of minutes. Pour glaze over fruit and chill to set.

YIELDS: 8 - 12 slices

Peach Gel with Raspberry Sauce

Naturally sweet, refreshing and simple to make. Equally grand with frozen peaches.

3½ c	**Pureed peaches (fresh or frozen)**
2	**Peaches, peeled and sliced**
1/4 c	**Agar flakes**
1/2 c	**Filtered water**
1 tsp	**Lemon juice**
1/2 c	**Apple or other juice**
1 recipe	**Raspberry Sauce (page 235)**

1. Put the pureed peaches into a medium bowl. Arrange the peach slices on the bottom of a pie dish in a spiraling circular pattern.
2. Dissolve the agar in the filtered water and juices, heat on high in a small saucepan until boiling, reduce and let bubble for 1 minute.
3. Pour the agar juice mixture into pureed peaches, stir or whisk together, then pour into the pie dish. (You can top with peaches if you don't want to invert the pie dish.) Chill for a minimum of 3 hours. Slice like a pie, and serve the *Raspberry Sauce* on top, or underneath the pie.

YIELDS: 6 - 8 servings

Perfect Papaya Pie

An extraordinarily beautiful and easy to make pie. Sliced papaya fills the Almond Pie Crust (page 223), and is accented with strawberries and bananas. A stunning pie to bring to gatherings or parties—you'll love it! Be sure to use ripe, firm papayas.

4	**Papayas, halved and seeded**
2	**Bananas, sliced on an angle**
1 c	**Strawberries, trimmed and halved**
1 recipe	**Almond Pie Crust**
1 recipe	**Vanilla Cashew Cream (page 235) for topping**

1. Prepare the pie crust and set it aside in the refrigerator. Slice each papaya halve into thin spears lengthwise, and remove the papaya skin.
2. Fill the pie crust with papaya spears, radiating out from the center. Put strawberries around the perimeter, flat side down. Next lay banana slices in the middle section. Place more papaya, or strawberry in the center.
3. Gently pack down fruit. Refrigerate if not serving right away. Slice to serve, topping each slice with *Vanilla Cashew Creme* (our mock whipped cream).

YIELDS: 8 servings

Pineapple Delight

Topped with Raspberry Applesauce, *this nonfat jelled dessert is quite a delight!*

2 c		Filtered water
3 Tbl		Agar flakes
1/2 tsp		Grated orange peel
2 tsp		Maple syrup
1 c		Pineapple, diced small
1		Banana, sliced
Topping:	1/2 c	Live Applesauce (page 72) mixed with
	1/2 c	Raspberry Sauce (page 235)

1. Stir together the filtered water and agar flakes in a small saucepan and bring it to a boil. After 1 minute, remove pan from the heat.
2. Mix together the orange zest, maple syrup, pineapple, and banana in a small bowl, and stir them into the agar pan. Spoon into 3 or 4 dessert cups and chill for 1 hour.
3. To serve: Unmold jelled dessert on dessert plates and spoon *Apple Raspberry Sauce* around dessert. Decorate with strawberry slices and a mint leaf.

YIELDS: 3 - 4 servings

Raspberry Bavarian Cream Pie

Raspberries and almond flavoring fill this un-fired pie.
Serve with a dollop of Vanilla Cashew Creme *(page 235).*

1¼ c		Red berry juice (divided use)
1 Tbl		Agar flakes
1 Tbl		Arrowroot powder
1/4 tsp		Almond extract
2 c		Raspberries
Cream layer:	1/2 c	Cashew pieces
	2 Tbl	Maple syrup
	1 c	Frozen berries
	1	Almond Pie Crust (page 223)

1. Whisk together 2/3 cup of the berry juice with the agar flakes and the arrowroot. Heat up on high in a small saucepan. Whisk for one minute until it thickens, then remove from heat. Whisk in the remaining juice and almond extract.
2. Put the berries into the raw pie crust, and pour the agar/juice mixture on top.
3. Blend "cream layer" ingredients together and pour over the pie. Freeze for half an hour before use. Decorate the top with extra berries before serving.

YIELDS: 6 - 8 servings

Raw Berry Pie

A simple, no-bake, fresh fruit torte. Serve with frozen Mango Cream (page 221), or other frozen fruit sorbets, or accent with Vanilla Cashew Creme (page 235).

1 basket	Strawberries, stems trimmed
1 basket	Raspberries
1 c	Fruit juice
1 Tbl	Agar flakes
1 recipe	Almond Pie Crust (page 223)

1. Trim and wash the berries, put them in paper towels to drain. Arrange on the *Almond Pie Crust.*
2. Mix the fruit juice with the agar flakes in a small pot, bring to a boil for 1 minute, then simmer for another minute. Let stand a couple of minutes before pouring over the fruit. Chill to set.

SERVES: 6

Almond Macadamia Fig Squares

Calmyrna figs are high in calcium, copper, manganese, magnesium, iron, and phosphorus. These are the best tasting fig squares around!

Crust:	1 c	Almonds, finely ground
	1/2	Vanilla bean, chopped
	1/2 c	Macadamia nuts, soaked (can substitute cashews)
	1 c	Dates, pitted
	1/3 c	Sprouted sunflower seeds
	2 c	Wheat sprouts
	1/2 c	Oat flakes, ground
Filling:	15	Calmyrna figs, soaked (in filtered water)

1. Grind the almonds with the chopped vanilla bean in two batches in a seed or nut mill. Put this ground almond-vanilla mixture into a food processor with the remaining crust ingredients. Pulse chop, pureeing well.
2. Press half of the crust mixture on the bottom of a lightly oiled rectangular pan.
3. Trim off the fig stems, puree the figs in a food processor. Spread the fig puree over the crust. Top with the remaining crust, pressing firmly and evenly. Top with sprinkles of oat flakes. Refrigerate till firm (overnight).
4. Cut into squares and place on food dehydrator trays. Dehydrate for about 10 hours. Delicious warm right out of the food dehydrator!

Apricot Pecan Drops

A soft, moist, and delicious cookie, especially good dehydrated with a banana slice on top.

1½ c	Soaked apricots, pitted
1 c	Pecans
1/2 c	Sprouted sunflower seeds
1/4 c	Dried apricots, chopped
1/4 tsp each	Cardamom and cinnamon
1/2 tsp	Vanilla

1. Pulse chop the pecans in a food processor. Add the remaining ingredients and blend them together.
2. Drop by spoonful onto lined food dehydrator trays. Flatten the cookie mixture onto the dehydrator trays with the back side of a spoon, or by pressing down a banana slice (or pecan half) on top of it.
3. Dehydrate for 10 hours, or until no longer wet.

YIELDS: 18 cookies

Banana Chews

These are our favorites! Follow the recipe for Sweet Energy Gems (page 233); however, add:

1/4 c   Ripe mashed banana to step #1

Press a banana slice 1/4˝ thick, onto each cookie before drying.

Carrot Cake Raisin Bars

A spicy, nutty bar made from sprouted wheat berries,
carrots and raisins. This savory loaf gets cut into bars and dehydrated until
moist and chewy. They keep for a long time if sealed and stored properly.
These also make a delicious snack or midmorning treat.

1½ c	**Carrot, finely grated**
2 c	**Sprouted wheat berries**
1/2 c	**Almonds, finely ground**
1/2 c	**Walnuts, ground**
1 tsp	**Cinnamon**
1/2 c	**Date paste**
1 tsp	**Vanilla**
1/4 tsp	**Cloves**
1/4 c	**Raisins**

1. Finely grate the carrots and set aside. Put the wheat berry sprouts, nuts, dates, and spices into a food processor and pulse chop into a paste.
2. Add the carrots and raisins into the wheat berry mixture and quickly pulse chop to mix (or stir in by hand).
3. Press the mixture into a lightly oiled small rectangular cake pan (7˝ × 9˝) and refrigerate overnight. Slice into bars (about 1½˝ × 3˝) and place on dehydrator trays. Dry for 24 hours. Serve hot out of the dehydrator with a banana based ice cream on top, or with a topping of *Prune Whip* (page 234).

YIELDS: 1 dozen

Crunchy Banana Log

A mixture of four dessert spices: vanilla, cardamon, nutmeg, and cinnamon make this banana "cake" extra delicious. Crunchy sprouted millet increases the nutritional value of this dessert, and the ground oats help hold together the moistness of the banana. This log gets rolled in shredded coconut for a pretty outrageous presentation.

2/3 c	**Banana, mashed**
2/3 c	**Almonds, ground**
2/3 c	**Oat flakes, ground**
1/2 tsp	**Cinnamon**
1 tsp	**Vanilla extract**
1/4 tsp each	**Cardamon and nutmeg**
3 Tbl	**Raisins**
1/2 c	**Sprouted millet**
Topping: 2 Tbl	**Coconut, shredded**

1. Pulse chop the bananas, almonds, and oats in a food processor. Add the spices and raisins and blend in well. Quickly pulse chop in the millet sprouts.
2. Spoon the mixture into a lightly oiled sheet of wax paper or foil. Tuck ends over the mixture then roll it up. Refrigerate for a few hours or overnight.
3. Unroll the log, then sprinkle coconut in front and roll log over to coat evenly with coconut. Slice with a wet knife to serve.

SERVING SUGGESTION:
Serve with a sauce of pureed frozen strawberries, thinned with orange juice.

Other Variations

Banana Pudding Crunch: To the above ingredients, add an extra 1/2 cup of mashed banana. Spoon into dessert cups after blending. Refrigerate if not serving immediately.

Crunchy Banana Cookies: Add an extra 1/2 cup of mashed banana to the ingredients. Instead of steps 2 and 3, spoon mixture onto lined food dehydrator trays and dry mixture for 8 to 10 hours.

SERVES: 6

New Mexican Fudgies

A date-sweetened sprouted wheat berry and carob cookie, "accented" with chile powder. The red chile gives a rich color and a warm flavor—delicious!

1 c	Sprouted soft wheat berries
1/3 c	Date "paste"
5 Tbl	Orange juice
1/3 c	Walnuts, minced
1 tsp	Vanilla
3 Tbl	Raw carob powder
1½ tsp	Red chile powder (New Mexican)

1. Pulse chop all of the ingredients (except the walnuts) in a food processor. Let the machine run in "on" position until pureed.
2. Stir in the walnuts, then drop by spoonful onto a lined dehydrator tray. Dehydrate for 10 to 12 hours.

YIELDS: 18 cookies

Orange Chews

Follow recipe for Sweet Energy Gems *(page 233) but blend in to the cookie dough:*

1 Tbl	Grated orange peel
1/2 Tbl	Orange juice

Follow steps 1 and 2 of *Sweet Energy Gems.*

Open Sesame Balls

Makes 18 sweet candies

1/2 c	Sesame tahini
1/4 c	Date pieces
1 Tbl	Carob powder
2 Tbl	Sesame seeds
2 Tbl	Coconut, shredded

1. Stir the first 4 goodies together and form into balls about 1˝ in diameter.
2. Roll the balls in coconut and refrigerate.

Sprouted Almond Croquettes
"The Healthiest Cookie Around"

A whole grain sprouted-wheat cookie. The natural sweetness comes from the maltose sugar in the sprouted wheat berries, with a little help from almond extract, currants and applesauce. Once you've sprouted the wheat berries, just grind the ingredients together for a delicious, crunchy fiber- and vitamin-rich treat. Using a food dehydrator to "bake" them preserves the vitamins, minerals, and enzymes.

1 c	Sprouted wheat berries
1/2 c	Live Applesauce (page 72)
1/3 c	Raw cashews
3/4 c	Currants
1/2 tsp	Almond extract
1/4 c	Almonds, minced

1. Pulse chop the sprouted wheat in a food processor, stop and scrape down the sides. Pulse chop in the applesauce and cashews, then add the currants and almond extract, blending for another 30 seconds.
2. Stir in the almonds and then drop the cookie dough by tablespoonful onto a lined food dehydrator tray. Flatten out the cookies, then dehydrate them for 12 hours, or until dry to the touch.

NOTE: You may wish to remove plastic wrap after 8 hours or so, once cookie dough has set. Continue dehydrating until firm, yet pliable.

YIELDS: 20 cookies

Sprouted Carob Cookies

A sprouted cookie naturally sweetened from the maltose sugar in the sprouted wheat, raisins, and the carob powder.

1 c	Sprouted wheat berries
1 tsp	Vanilla
1/3 c	Raw cashews (or soaked in filtered water)
1/3 c	Unsweetened coconut flakes (optional)
1/4 c	Raw carob powder
1/3 c	Soaked raisins (soak in filtered water to soften)

1. Grind the sprouted wheat berries in a food processor with the vanilla and the cashews. Stop and scrape down the sides. Puree to a paste.
2. Add the coconut and the carob powder, and pulse chop again. Pulse chop in the raisins for 3 seconds.
3. Roll between your wet palms into 1˝ balls, flatten onto a plastic-wrap lined food dehydrator tray. Dehydrate for about 12 hours.

YIELDS: 21 cookies

Sweet Energy Gems

A date sweetened, sprouted sunflower seed cookie that "bakes" in the food dehydrator, creating a high-energy treat!

3/4 c	**Dates, packed, pitted**
2 c	**Sprouted sunflower seeds**
1 tsp	**Cinnamon**
1 tsp	**Vanilla extract**

1. Pulse chop all of the ingredients in a food processor until well combined.
2. Press spoonfuls of the cookie dough* onto lined food dehydrator trays. Dehydrate for 10 to 14 hours.

NOTE: You may wish to speed drying time by removing the tray liners once the cookie is dry on the outer edges, so that the hot air can dry the bottom of the cookie.

*Cookies can be topped with walnuts or raisins, or strawberry or kiwi slices before drying.

YIELDS: 3 dozen

Sweet Oat Crisps

Delicious thin cookies. Serve alone or on the side of a frozen fruit ice cream.

1 c	**Rolled oats (you can use multi-grain flakes, too)**
2/3 c	**Hot filtered water**
1/2 c	**Sprouted wheat berries**
2 Tbl	**Orange juice**
1 Tbl	**Date paste**
1/2 tsp	**Cinnamon**

Blend all of the ingredients in a blender until pureed. Pour into small circles or shapes onto lined food dehydrator trays. Dehydrate for about 10 hours or until crisp.

Apple Cream

*Cashews and applesauce blend to create a creamy topping
on fruit salads or desserts.*

1/2 c	Raw cashews
1 c	Live Applesauce (page 72)
2 Tbl	Maple syrup
Dash	Cinnamon

Pulse chop all of the ingredients in a food processor, then blend them to a smooth, creamy consistency.

YIELDS: 1¼ cups

Carob Sauce

*A delicious sauce over fresh fruit "ice creams"
or as a dip for bananas, apples or pears.*

4 Tbl	Carob powder
1/2 c	Almond Milk (page 57)
2 tsp	Tahini
1 tsp	Vanilla extract
2 tsp	Maple syrup

Whisk together the carob powder and the *Almond Milk* in a small bowl until smooth. Stir in the remaining ingredients. Refrigerate.

YIELDS: 2/3 cup

Prune Whip

*Use as a delectable topping to müesli, oatmeal, fruit, and desserts.
Or, serve it as is, it makes a wonderful pudding.*

14	Soaked prunes
1/2 c	Soak water (filtered water)
1/4 c	Cashews
2 Tbl	Orange juice
1/2 tsp	Cinnamon

Blend all of the ingredients in a blender until smooth.

YIELDS: About 1/2 cup or 2 pudding cups

Raspberry Sauce

*Spoon over cakes or nondairy ice creams, or
serve on the bottom of a slice of cake for a fruity accent to desserts.*

1½ c	**Frozen raspberries**
4 Tbl	**Fruit juice**
1 Tbl	**Pineapple juice concentrate or maple syrup**

Puree the raspberries in a food processor until smooth, add the fruit juice to attain the desired consistency.

Vanilla Cashew Creme

*This is our mock whipped cream made from cashews and dates. A wonderful
topping on desserts or over fresh cut fruits. Use like whipped cream.*

1 c	**Raw cashew pieces, soaked in filtered water**
1/3 c	**Pitted dates, soaked in filtered water**
1/2 tsp	**Vanilla**

1. Strain the water from the cashews and put the cashews into a blender and grind.
2. Add the dates and some of their soak water to the blender, along with the vanilla, then puree well until creamy and fluffy. Store in a small container in the fridge.

How to Make Dried Lemon or Orange Zest

Make your own delicious dried lemon or orange peel by saving the skins of organic lemons or oranges. Wash and dry the peel, then shave off the outer layer of the rind (colored part only) with a knife or vegetable peeler. To dry the peel, place it in the bottom tray of a food dehydrator for 24 to 48 hours or until crispy. Then place in a food grinder and pulverize into a fine powder. Store in a glass jar.

30 Days of Vibrant Meals

On the following pages we offer to you a colorful palette of menus from which you can create your perfect live foods diet, balancing tastes, textures, quantities of food, and frequency of meals.

Envision your daily meal preparations as a celebration of Life's Banquet!

	DAY 1	DAY 2	DAY 3
Breakfast	Pineapple Date Shake	Hummingbird's Buzz Smoothie	Peaches and Cream
Lunch	Tomato Corn Jubilee Rye Crisps Seasoned Nut Cheese	Cracked Wheat Jubilee	Hawaiian Pineapple Boats
Dinner	Sweet Potato Hiziki "Pasta" Salad Small Leafy Green Salad with Olive Garlic Vinaigrette	Thai Broccoli Salad Spicy Sprout Salad Sweet-Ziki	Cauliflower Seed Cheese Loaf Lemon Tahini Sauce Curried Carrot Kraut
Dessert	Peach Gel with Raspberry Sauce	Strawberry Nut Ice Cream	Raspberry Bavarian Cream Pie

Please refer to the alphabetical index which is found at the back of this book for the page numbers of these recipes.

	DAY 4	DAY 5	DAY 6
Breakfast	Cinnamon Apple Cracked Wheat Cereal	Müesli with Berries	Sprouted Wheat and Date Loaf Prune Whip Herbal Tea
Lunch	Jicama Kiwi Salad Cranberry Gingerales	Fresh Fruit Kabobs with Avonana Sauce	Orange and Fennel Salad Kiwiberry Soup
Dinner	Tabouli Spinach Salad Creamy Tomato Soup	Marvelous Orange Asparagus Salad Garden Ginger Energy Soup	Beet Polarity Soup Classic Dilly Kraut Marinated Cucumbers
Dessert	Fresh Fruit Ring with Vanilla Cashew Cream	Carrot Cake Raisin Bars French Vanilla Herbal Tea	Orange Chews Bengal Spice Tea

	DAY 7	DAY 8	DAY 9
Breakfast	Royal Applesauce with Banana Chips	Vibrant Oatmeal with Live Applesauce	Papaya Kiwi Salad with Avonana Sauce
Lunch	California Nori Rolls	Wild West Pineapple Salad	Seed Cheese Cabbage Rolls Carrot Sticks
Dinner	Fennel Cabbage Slaw Yam Patties Peanut Sauce	Leafy Green and Sprout Salad Lentil Almond Log	Red Onion Pickles Delphi Spinach Salad Sprouted Wheat Thins Pesto of Choice
Dessert	Just Peachy Peppermint Tea	New Mexican Fudgies Romaccinos	Pineapple Delight

	DAY 10	DAY 11	DAY 12
Breakfast	Golden Mandala	Sapote Exoticus	Pink Hawaiian Smoothie
Lunch	Hearty Lentil Soup Chard Ribbon Salad	Curried Peach Bisque Nefertiti's Carrot Salad	Creamy Tomato Soup Vegetable Seed Cheese Sprouted Rye Crisps
Dinner	Gazpacho Fiesta Coleslaw with Avocado Sauce Sprouted Wheat Thins	Green Bean Tomato Salad Herb Crackers Dream de la Cream Spread	Pandora's Salad Carrot Cleanser
Dessert	Piña Colada Sorbet	Crunchy Banana Log with Raspberry Sauce	Raw Berry Pie

	DAY 13	**DAY 14**	**DAY 15**
Breakfast	Tropical Mint Julep	Magic Müesli	Froggy's Quantum Leap Smoothie
Lunch	Vibrant Pink Salad	Papaya Lime Salad	Independence Day Salad
Dinner	Japanese Buddhist's Delight Lunafish Sushi	English Garden Tomato Ring Arugula Spinach Salad	Black Bean Fiesta Salad Awesome Guacamole
Dessert	Orange Slices	Fresh Fruit Tart Herbal Tea	Purple Mint Passion

	DAY 16	DAY 17	DAY 18
Breakfast	Raspberry Almond Parfait	Pink Tropic	Maui Mango Delight
Lunch	Sunshew Spread Stuffed Tomato Grated Beet Salad	Sprouted Lentil Spread rolled in Lettuce Leaf "Tacos" and Sprouts	Red Pepper Arugula Rolls Carrot Classic
Dinner	Sea Pasta Vegetable Salad Veggie Delight Juice	Imperial Salad	Large Mandala Salad Millet Burgers with Cheezy Cashew Sauce
Dessert	Cherimoya Freeze	Strawberry Orange Sorbet	Almond Macadamia Fig Squares French Vanilla Tea

	DAY 19	DAY 20	DAY 21
Breakfast	Creamy Monkey Smoothie	Cinnamon Apple Cracked Wheat Cereal	Apple Raisin Müesli
Lunch	Confetti Salad Sweet Potato Chips	California Nori Rolls Almond Corn Wowder	Zucchini Bisque Seed Cheese stuffed Red Pepper Wedges with Sprouts
Dinner **Dessert**	Sweet Golden Salad Cottage "Seed" Cheese Sprouted Wheatzas	Italian Deli Salad Garden Crisps with Besto Pesto Cottage "Seed" Cheese	Spicy Chile Beans Salsa Fresca
	Apricot Pecan Drops Herbal Tea	Banana Almandine Cream Sweet Oat Crisps	Pink Pineapple Whip

	DAY 22	DAY 23	DAY 24
Breakfast	Persimmon Ecstasy	A Fruitful Breakfast OR Watermelon Lime Juice	Caramel Breakfast Apple Pudding
Lunch	Curried Waldorf Salad Apple Lemon Juice	Borscht Hot House Cucumber Almond Salad	Cantaloupe Flower Salad Iced Herbal Tea
Dinner	Alfalfa Fennel Soup Fleur de Broccoli Sweet-Ziki	Sweet Potato "Pasta" Tomato Basil Sauce	Ruby Beet Loaf Salad topped with Savory Seeds
Dessert	Sweet Energy Gems Herbal Tea	Perfect Papaya Pie	Banana Splits with Carob Sauce

	DAY 25	DAY 26	DAY 27
Breakfast	Magic Müesli	Multi-grain Strawberry Müesli	Cantaloupe Cleanser
Lunch	French Bean Salad Cucumber Bisque	Seasprout Salad Rolls Carrot Classic	Super "C" Salad Sweet Oat Crisps
Dinner	Curried Tomato Cups Cumin Cabbage Slaw Jicama Sticks	Ruby Ginger Kraut Minced Cauliflower Salad Seasoned Nut Cheese	Oriental Barley Salad Aramesk and Sprouts
Dessert	Sliced Pears with Carob Sauce	Sprouted Almond Croquettes	Mango Cream

	DAY 28	DAY 29	DAY 30
Breakfast **Lunch**	Orange Banana Flips	Sliced Bananas and Strawberries Carrot Cake Raisin Bars Herbal Tea	Elephant Spread Sprouted Wheat and Date Loaf Fresh Pressed Orange Juice
Dinner	Honolulu Tossed Salad	Delphi Spinach Salad with Seasoned Seed Cheese Fresh Carrot Juice	Sweet Golden Salad with Spicy Cucumber Garden Dressing Rejuvenating Lemonade
Dessert	Yalmond Spread stuffed Bell Pepper halves Tomato Corn Jubilee	Carrot Lentil Burgers with Peanut Sauce on a small bed of Alfalfa Sprouts Vibrant Pink Salad with Tahiso Dressing	Grated Sweet Potato "Pasta" served with Creamy Pesto Sauce Salad of Baby Greens and Sprouts with Tomato Basil Dressing
	Open Sesame Balls Giinseng Blend Herbal Tea	Cherimoya Freeze	Aphrodite's Freeze

Quick Meal Ideas

Combine these recipes for great meals

MORNING MEALS:
- Have *Prune Whip* over banana, orange, and apple slices
- Pour *Avonana Sauce* over 1/2 papaya filled with sliced bananas
- Serve *Creamy Soaked Seed Sauce* over a bowl of mixed berries: "Berries 'n Cream"

EVENING MEALS:
- Toss *Pecan Basil Pesto* into finely shredded carrots, yams or sweet potatoes: "Pecan Basil Pesto with Vegetable 'Pasta' "
- Stuff a tomato shell with cubed avocado and shredded carrots, top with *Cheezy Cashew Sauce.*
- Put *Lunafish Salad Spread on* top of a lengthwise half of a cucumber that has been seeded: "Lunafish Cucumber Boats"
- For a "Santa Fe Salad," stir *Red Chile Sauce into* cut corn, chopped peppers, and minced zucchini
- Stuff spinach leaves with *Cosmic Red Pepper Spread* and serve with *Lemon Tahini Sauce* or *Creamy Soaked Seed Sauce*
- Stuff a half of a papaya that has been seeded with *Sunshew Spread* and top with *Pyramid Sauce*: "Tropical Pyramid"

SNACKS:
- Put *Spicy Peanut Spread* in yellow, green, and red pepper ribs
- Dehydrate *Tomato Chutney Sauce on* eggplant slices
- Stuff mushroom caps with *Besto Pesto* or *Greek Olive Pesto*
- Roll *Vegetable Seed Cheese* in bibb lettuce or spinach leaves
- Put *Sprouted Lentil Spread in* the ribs of celery
- Slice a small avocado in half and fill with *Salsa Fresco* or *Pineapple Salsa*

DESSERTS:
- Mix strawberries in soaked seed sauce, use this strawberry seed sauce ecstasy to fill an *Almond Pie Crust* for "Strawberry Short Cake"
- Dip peeled bananas in *Carob Sauce* and freeze for a "Frozen Carob Banana"

Seed Cheese and Yogurt Variations:

Culturing seed and nut sauces with exciting combinations of vegetables, herbs, and spices enhances the overall flavor of your fermented seed yogurts or cheeses.

Here are a few suggestions for savory combos:

♥ *"Pink Celebration Sauce"*: Blend a small chopped beet, 2 garlic cloves, and 2 tsp miso into your *Basic Sun Almond Cheese* before letting it "culture" on your counter for 6 to 8 hours. Serve as a salad dressing or sauce.

♥ *"Harvest Cheese"*: Fall flavors of thyme, leeks, and oregano enhance this seed cheese. Follow the *Basic Sun Almond Cheese* recipe; however, substitute walnut pieces for the sunflower seeds. Add 1 tsp each of thyme and oregano, 2 garlic cloves, 1/2 cup chopped leeks, 1/2 tsp of cordiander, and 1/4 cup of fresh parsley leaves to the blender along with the soaked nuts. Culture as directed. Spoon into a cheesecloth, twist tightly and hang mixture over a bowl for 8 hours. Slice and serve "cheese" with dehydrated crackers or salads.

♥ *"Sweet Cinnamon Seed Yogurt"*: To the *Basic Sun Almond Cheese* recipe, add 2 tsp of cinnamon, 1/4 cup of date paste, and 1/2 tsp of orange rind to the blender along with the soaked nuts. Ferment only 4 to 6 hours. Serve with fruits or dessert.

Alphabetical Index

Celebrate Your Wellness

To order additional copies of

Vibrant Living

at $14.95* each

or to order our other Heart Healthy,
fully illustrated cookbooks,

A Vegetarians Ecstasy

and

A Celebration of Wellness

at $14.95* each

Call GLO, INC.

1-800-854-2587

USA NATIONWIDE AND CANADA

VISA AND MASTERCARD ACCEPTED

**ALL CREDIT CARD ORDERS
SHIPPED WITHIN 48 HOURS!**

*PLUS $2 SHIPPING AND HANDLING, AND STATE TAX WHERE APPLICABLE.

- -

TO ORDER BY MAIL:

Send to GLO, INC.
2406 FIFTH AVENUE
SAN DIEGO, CA 92101

Please send me:

_____ copies of *A Vegetarians Ecstasy* @ $14.95* each $_____

_____ copies of *A Celebration of Wellness* @ $14.95* each $_____

_____ copies of *Vibrant Living* @ $14.95* each $_____

Add $2 shipping and handling per book $_____

California residents add 7.75% sales tax: $_____
  (*A Vegetarians Ecstasy* add $1.16 per book)
  (*A Celebration of Wellness* add $1.16 per book)
  (*Vibrant Living* add $1.16 per book)

TOTAL AMOUNT ENCLOSED $_____

SHIPPING ADDRESS:

NAME_____
          FIRST   LAST

ADDRESS_____
                   NO & STREET

CITY_____STATE_____ZIP_____

PHONE (IN CASE WE HAVE A QUESTION) (_____)_____